Tormented Voices

Tormented Voices

Power, Crisis, and Humanity
in Rural Catalonia

1140–1200

THOMAS N. BISSON

Harvard University Press
Cambridge, Massachusetts
London, England
1998

Library of Congress Cataloging-in-Publication Data

Bisson, Thomas N.
Tormented voices : power, crisis, and humanity in rural Catalonia, 1140–1200 /
Thomas N. Bisson.
p. cm.
Includes bibliographical references and index.
ISBN 0–674–89527–4 (cloth : alk. paper).
ISBN 0–674–89528–2 (pbk. : alk. paper)
1. Peasantry—Spain—Catalonia—Social conditions.
2. Power (Social sciences)—Spain—Catalonia.
3. Catalonia (Spain)—Civilization.
4. Catalonia (Spain)—Rural conditions.
5. Violence—Spain—Catalonia—History.
I. Title.
HD1536.S7B57 1998
305.5′633′09467—dc21   97-46083

Preface

I have tried to evoke some people who happened to live in villages, fields, and pastures under the lordship of the Count of Barcelona about 850 years ago. Their freedoms and prosperity were coming under pressure in an age of competitive growth. They survive today only in some little-known records of their complaints against a few other people whom they served, obeyed, and feared. Problematic and mostly unpublished, these records are partial as well as few in number. I have tried to learn from them, even to imagine from them, without misreading them. For I have lived with them enough to be persuaded that, whatever their limitations, they afford rare evidence of how power was experienced in a medieval peasant society.

That is the subject, more exactly, of my evocation. I have ventured into the contexts of that historical experience without straying far beyond the testimony of my chosen few sources. So the result is considerably less than a history of peasants, or even of all the rulers' tenants, and very much less than one of power in medieval Catalonia. These are grand themes for bigger books. But they are themes that can only be enriched by microhistorical investigation of some of their more resonant and least explored sources. What I have attempted is an essay in compassionate history.

Whether it works, or even persuades, we shall see; I have only tried to understand. I have wrung people from their names; listened for their voices in words, sometimes their own, that give life to tenuous recollection; have clung to these people in their assertions of violence and suffering. Who were they? What happened to them? What did it mean? The understanding I have wished to reconstruct in and about them cannot be complete, given the ravages of time and my own limitations, but I believe it has historical truth.

The book seeks to be "user-friendly" without compromising the fresh air of the twelfth century. My reason for naming peasants just as their scribes did long ago is explained on pages 58, 157. Technical terms are clarified or translated in a Glossary. Specialist readers need perhaps only be reminded that the memorials of complaint (as I shall call them) survive in diverse historical contexts by no means fully studied here; that my results will surely be improved when one day—no easy task—a critical and indexed edition of these documents is produced.

This book has spun out of research and teaching on power and cultural change. The memorials of complaint are related to the early fiscal records I examined in *Fiscal Accounts of Catalonia under the Early Count-Kings (1151–1213)*, 2 vols. (Berkeley, 1984). Some of the substance of Chapter III was written for a conference at Girona (Catalonia) in 1985 and was then published as "The Crisis of the Catalonian Franchises 1150–1200)," cited fully on page 5, n. 5. For help in securing photographs to reproduce, I thank my friends Rvd. Dr. Antoni Pladevall i Font, Mn. Gabriel Roura, Dra. Teresa Matas i Blanxart, Dr. Joan-F. Cabestany i Fort (the latter two in the Centre d'Art Romànic Català, Barcelona), Dra. Immaculada Ollich i Castanyer, and Professor Frederic Udina Martorell. Dr. Enrique Alonso García negotiated the agreement with the Ministerio de Educación y Cultura that made it possible to represent some of the documents on which the book is based. Professor Manuel Mundó i Marcet scaled the heights of Font-rubí and Argençola with me on a dizzying day in which we also pursued the tormentors of those places to their lairs in Mediona and Clariana. I reiterate my thanks to the John Simon Guggenheim Memorial Foundation for supporting the work of 1964–1965 when I first encountered these records. Harvard's Faculty of Arts and Sciences has generously supported my latest research. And while this is quite a personal book, perhaps more deeply my own than is prudent, other people have kindly tried it out with me: friends, colleagues, students, my family. Bernard Bailyn and Simon Schama helped me to frame it in wider perspectives. Teofilo F. Ruiz and Robert J. Brentano made welcome suggestions, encouraging me to reconsider, to do better. As for those people of long ago, they gripped me. The inspiration was there, ever the subject of my dedication.

TNB

Contents

Illustrations

(following p. 67)

Flight into Egypt. Santa Maria of Estany; capital sculpture, late twelfth century.

Memorial of Gavà, Sant Climent, and Viladecans, c. 1145–1150. Original, ACA, Cancelleria, pergamins extrainventaris 3451. Courtesy of the Ministerio de Educación y Cultura. Archivo de la Corona de Aragón.

Memorial of Corró (d'Avall), c. 1162–1170. Original, ACA, Canc., perg. extrainv. 3214. Courtesy of the Ministerio de Educación y Cultura. Archivo de la Corona de Aragón.

Argençola, from the northeast. Photograph by permission of Enciclopèdia catalana, S.A.

"Tapestry of Creation," late eleventh century. Cathedral Treasury, Girona. Reproduced by permission of the Cathedral Church of Girona.

"Summer" *(Estas)*, from "Tapestry of Creation" (Girona). Reproduced by permission of the Cathedral Church of Girona.

Rachel and her flock. Santa Maria of Girona, capital sculpture, twelfth century. Reproduced by permission of the Centre d'Art Romànic Català.

Nor you, ye Proud, impute to These the fault,
If Memory o'er their Tomb no Trophies raise.

—*Thomas Gray*

[I]

MEMORIALS

The people died long ago. *Oliba, Arnaldus Ademar, Geralla. . . .* They must all have been dead by 1200, most of them doubtless by then long since. Their very memory was buried with them and their children; no one built monuments to them. *Martinus, Gitarda uidua* (widow), *Petrus Iohanis. . . .* Only their names, it seemed, survived in written records as useless to later generations as the familial memories were fragile; that is, names deprived of memory, of context. In reality, something else came with those names: the voices of these people. Stilled, fading out, and forgotten among the living, their voices survived like some distant signal from the deep; and survived, again like a signal, encoded. I could not read the code when the records first lay before me, let alone hear the voices. Even today much remains baffling about the tired photocopies juxtaposed in reticent reenactment of an intellectual reception many years ago in Barcelona's (old) Archive of the Crown of Aragon. "From *Petrus Dagberti* .xiii. Stole R de r from *petrus pardines* .v. sl. . . ." Names, numbers, allegations stare back defiantly like the staccato bits of digital electronic language. But I see now less dimly, or hear in what I read, something more than letters and words; hear something pulsing, pulsing out of the lives and predicaments of people who by the cruel dictates of time and corrup-

tion should be no more than names to us, or sums. "Oh Lord
Count Raimund . . . give back to us the land we live in, that we
may be yours!"[1]

Voice, voices, voiced humanity in rolling lands folded between
the Pyrenees Mountains and the Mediterranean Sea. Inert names
stir in these voices, but it is in their resonant passion, and especially
in their misfortunes, that these people speak, or even cry out, to us.
"And he took from me .xxvii. small animals and seized my
crops. . . ." So said *Amallus de Valoria*—and so in their different
ways did countless others. It is easy to sympathize with them, less
easy to understand them. It looks as if *Amallus* had a good deal to
lose. His was an account of what he was owed as well as an allegation. Moreover, the speechless tormentors surely took a different
view of things; they did well in all but reputation. Put on notice by
voiced suffering, we may reasonably hope to discover something of
unvoiced prosperity. The names, ever cryptic and stark, become
more engaging; stand out from the mass more clearly than on first
sight. *Guilelma de planes. Amallus Rog.*[2]

The names and voices come first and last. They have a story to
tell. I shall try to find the people in the names in the next chapter,
to evoke something of their village habitats, to imagine their ways
of life. Their witness, their sufferings, their voices will be the subjects thereafter. And if these are well heard, something of his and
her stories run together—something of history—will come into
view; for whatever we make of the singular evidence on which this
book rests, it will be found in accord with sources less problematic,
more abundant, and themselves still little investigated. The villagers
of Old Catalonia in the middle of the twelfth century were
beneficiaries and (more commonly) victims of new social and eco-

1. See Appendix 1 on Usage, Citations and Abbreviations (p. 158). The records are identified and discussed in this chapter, pp. 6–26; and are numbered and
described in Appendix 4. Those cited in this paragraph are, in this order: Tts3283,
C-Ll-2501, F2-3141, R1-3433, F1-3409.
2. Co3214, C-Ll-2501, Ter3275.

nomic forces they can hardly have understood, still less have con-
trolled. This is a book about those people, or rather, about some of
them. About *Petrus Gitard, Adalyde de Perpiniano,* and also about the
men and women—Arnal de Perella, Berenguer de Bleda, the Lady
lord of Mediona among others—who tormented them.[3]

It is also a book about our experience, about what we know or can
hope to know, of a small world in the distant past. The people and
their voices and story will engage us, but I begin with the memorials made for their lords, the counts of Barcelona, which bring them
to us. For they are part of a history that can only have meaning for
us and they are the part we can know best. It may seem odd to
speak of "memorials" given my claim that no one built monuments
to these people. What we have of this remembrance, to speak more
exactly, is a fortuitous survival of memoranda, of helps to ever
failing memories. Serving needs of their moment, these records
took no interest in the future. Moreover, unlike modern memoranda from which historians can compile records of events in time,
the ones here of interest float in timeless space. Not one of them is
dated. At best we can recognize a familiar incident or two from
laconic allusions. These are records written for people who, knowing already what most mattered, needed only to assemble the details which they themselves could soon safely forget. This is why—
final disgrace!—not even the writers of our documents are usually
known. Nothing more was needed of them but the writing of what
they heard. The writings may well have been put to use, in occasions about which we may plausibly guess but which are otherwise
unknown to history.

So we are dealing virtually with orphans. Do orphans not bear

3. R1-3433, C-Ll-2501, F1-3 (3409, 3141, 3288). The related sources are to
be found in *DI,* iv (1849); *LFM;* ACA, Cancelleria, pergamins Ramon Berenguer
IV, Alfons I, and extrainventaris; plus multiplying editions of the records of ecclesiastical patrimonies, conveniently listed by Jordi Fernandez Cuadrench and Pierre
Bonnassie in a report to appear in *Le Moyen Age* (1997).

the memory? We should know better. That is why I prefer to regard these memoranda as memorials and to think of the impulse that created them as located in peasant societies whose anonymous interrogators could not fail to be affected. Scribes in southern France and the Pyrenees labeled some of their products "memorial charters" or the like, and we shall see how this usage affected our pieces.[4] But there was nothing to prevent jottings of any description or none at all from transcending the absolutely forgettable, from being touched by common humanity. And that is what seems to have happened to some of the undated parchments that survived in the archives of the count-kings of Barcelona.

The ones that reach out to me. Let me concede at once that most of the extant pieces that are anonymous and undated are devoid of such traces. This is why the whole class has been sadly neglected by historians. Taken piece by piece, this collection of several hundred parchments is so perplexing that it remains little known and less used to this day; nor (in a sense) can it finally hold much interest for us, because we know that it was put together out of the debris of the classified records centuries after the lifetimes of our villagers by bewildered archivists unable to place the pieces chronologically. But amongst these parchments are two subgroups of pieces that do matter here: first, a batch of inventories of lords' domains known generically as "briefs" (brevia) or (in singular number) "head of brief" (caput brevis; Catalan: capbreu); second, a batch of records of complaint about alleged malfeasance by lords, knights, and officials; the word "complaint(s)" (querimonia-e) typically figures in these documents. That the first of these groups survived is hardly surprising: descriptions of domains might go out of date but would seldom have been superseded outright. Capbreus might or might not be dated, so the absence of dates in this subset would presumably have been less troublesome to clerks in the medieval

---

4. *Les plus anciennes chartes en langue provençale* . . ., ed. Clovis Brunel (Paris, 1926), nos. 62, 75, 89, 91, 92, 95.

archives than to their modern successors. But there was less reason, indeed no obvious reason at all, to retain the records of complaint. Even if written complaints were (once) produced before count's or count-king's officials, their moment passed. The names and their charges would soon have been forgotten, leaving useless records far from the local scenes they evoked. Neither *capbreus* nor complaints were of any interest to the clerks who began to copy existing original records of castles toward 1180. They wrote on the back of one fiscal list: "*caput breue,* and we don't know whose or when. Not copied." They cast it aside—but they kept it.[5]

"Not copied," nor were they ever copied before our times. What we have are parchment originals which keep their secrets. Some of them, indeed most, I shall trouble no more. Of about 100 "uninventoried parchments" in the Archive of the Crown of Aragon with the potential to reveal something about village life in the twelfth century, I have dismissed all but sixteen. These are the "orphans," wild-eyed in their clear bright inks but unfrightened, most likely to respond to questioning. All but one are from the subset of complaints, although two others—"this is a brief of many evils . . ." and "this is a commemoration of bad deeds . . ."—are of

5. On the genre *caput brevis,* see Pere Benito i Monclús, "*Hoc est breve . . .* L'emergència del costum i els orígens de la pràctica de capbreviació (segles XI–XIII)," *Estudios sobre renta, fiscalidad y finanzas en la Cataluña bajomedieval,* ed. Manuel Sánchez Martínez. Anuario de Estudios medievales, Anejo 27 (Barcelona, 1993), pp. 3–27; for complaints, see Pierre Bonnassie, *La Catalogne du milieu du Xe à la fin du XIe siècle. Croissance et mutations d'une société,* 2 vols. (Toulouse, 1975–76), ii, 615, 730, 736; Blanca Garí, "Las *querimoniae* feudales en la documentación catalana del siglo XII (1131–1178)," *Medievalia* v (1984), 7–49; and Josep M. Salrach, "Agressions senyorials i resistències pageses en el procés de feudalització (segles IX–XII)," *Revoltes populars contra el poder de l'estat.* (Barcelona, 1992), pp. 11–29 (esp. 20–28); and for more information on the records pertinent to this book, T. N. Bisson, "The Crisis of the Catalonian Franchises (1150–1200)," *La formació i expansió del feudalisme català.* Actes del Col.loqui organitzat pel Col.legi Universitari de Girona (8–11 de gener de 1985), ed. Jaume Portella i Comas. Estudi General no. 5–6 (Girona, 1986), pp. 155–157. The quoted dorsal notation is found in ACA, Cancelleria, pergamins extrainv. 3247.

manifestly mixed parentage.[6] I shall not hesitate to consult others beyond my select sixteen when that seems useful, but information culled from these chosen witnesses will be the basis for my conclusions.

A further consideration in justification of this method may be useful. Very few in the larger pool of undated parchments are related to one another in respect to persons, situations, and locales. These are not merely orphans; they're not even relations, let alone siblings. So there seems little to be gained by multiplying raw data from these sources, and something perhaps to be lost to confusion. In any case, I have included the rare sets of related parchments, or most of them, among my chosen sixteen; and I have drawn upon related evidence for all the situations which produced the sixteen, wherever it is to be found.

So let me introduce these survivors, to themselves, as it were, as well as to us. I have come to like them, reticent or even truculent though some of them are, which is why I imagine them as people with *their* own stories to tell. But you who read this, how could I entice you to like them without magically multiplying them as originals, perhaps stuffed in pouches at the back of this book; or (less fantastically) without quietly assembling them on a table in Barcelona with all of us sitting there? Even then some readers might find them less than sparkling company, leaving me an embarrassed host seeing friends early to the door. For while we can greet them in their shabby clothes, front and back; can "size them up," so to speak (in millimeters, as scholars do; see Appendix 4); and can even "read" them in a sense: for all this, we cannot coax out of them what exactly they did before they retired from active life. Collectively, they have a story which I have already narrated in brief, that of the detention camps through which they have passed.

6. C-Ll-2501, E-G29. I classify all but Tts3283 as complaints.

Taken one by one, they seem all too like artifacts pulled from drawers.

Let me hold to the life in them. What matters here is the senses of locale, of people remembered in the memorials, and of parentage (if I may speak so of the scribes who wrote them). To review the memorials in something like the order in which they were written will be to pay first visits to some places that will become familiar and to greet some of the people whose remembrance comes only with these parchments. Because the chronology is far from certain and because four of the localities are represented by two or more memorials, I have thought it useful to group the subsets for the villages of Caldes, Llagostera, Esclet, and Ganix (they are numbered 4 and 5 in Appendix 4, where a list and technical descriptions of the pieces will be found), for Font-rubí (nos. 6–8), for the Ribes valley (nos. 11, 12), and for Cabra del Camp (nos. 14, 15).

My first witness speaks crisply from the fertile plain beneath Mount Canigou in the French Pyrenees. "Recognition," it says, "of the maintenance [*alberga*] which the Count ought to have in Terrats. *Arnaldus Garriga* owes maintenance for three knights and three squires plus two sextars of feedgrain." *Raimundus Gunter* owes the same, and so do *Martinus, Berengerius,* and four other men. *Arnaldus Ademar* owes a half-*alberga*, *Wilelmus barun* something less than that, while *Wilelmus* the bailiff is said to owe *alberga* for six knights, six squires plus four sextars of feedgrain,—that is, double-maintenance. "This aforesaid *alberga* the Count has in Terrats and has absolutely no other imposition." That's all: eight lines of script in a bright large hand; the obligations of eleven peasant householders to lodge their Lord-Count, on whose behalf a scribe listed them with laconic economy. No detail was unnecessarily repeated; where he could, the scribe wrote "the same" (*similiter*).

This record lights up the reality of Pyrenean power as in a flash

FRANCE

Perpignan
Terrats • Elne

ROUSSILLON

R. Tet

PYRENEES

CERDANYA

La Seu
d'Urgell

Queralbs
Fustanya • • Pardines
Ribes

ARAGON

Organyà

Besalú

OLD CATALONIA

R. Fluvià

R. Ter

Girona

Vic • •
Valmala

Caldes de
Malavella • Esclet
• • Ganix
Llagostera

VALLÈS

Corró d'Avall

Lleida

Argençola • •
Clariana

Terrassa

Bell-lloc

Mediterranean Sea

Mediona • •

Castellví

Font-rubí
Cabra
Vilafranca •

St. Climent
de Llobregat
Viladecans •
Gavà •

Barcelona

N

PENEDÈS

Tarragona

CATALONIA

Locations of Rural Complaint

1140–1200

0   10   20   30   40   50
miles
0 10 20 30 40 50 60 70 80
km

‡ Archbishopric
† Bishopric
• Domain or village
• Hamlet
▲ Castle

of sunlight. Terrats, a village located fifteen miles southwest of
Perpignan, was not the possession of the Lord-Count of Roussillon, who would have had small need of hospitality in domains so
close to his own strongholds. It was the Count of Barcelona with
his retinue of mounted (and armed) knights and squires, descending

the River Tech from the Vallespir on his way to Provence, or preparing for the mountain-crossing on return, who exploited this lordship at Terrats. Thanks to dated records referring to these very hospitalities, which were sometimes commended in fief to other men, the memorial of Terrats can be placed late in the reign of Count Raimund Berenguer III (1096–1131) or soon thereafter.[7]

It does not, I must admit, much resemble its fellow survivors. It is not on its face a memorial of complaints, for no one is represented as aggrieved. But neither is it a simply a *capbreu,* for the interest in lordly entitlement is more than offset by that of "recognizing" a limit on specific obligations. So the question arises: on whose initiative was this "recognition" produced? Can't we hear something still, some overtone, of a negotiation such as was absolutely concealed in the stark impersonality of most *capbreus?* "This *alberga* has the Count in Terrats and absolutely no other imposition."

Roussillon will fall silent hereafter. Not for lack of evidence of the same harsh lordship suffered in the villages next to be considered, but the counts of Barcelona had limited interests north of the Pyrenees before one of them annexed Roussillon in 1172, and the native counts made no such effort to remedy violence as the memorials of Barcelona indicate.

The next two records in likely order come from the vicinity of Barcelona city. Dating from about 1145 to 1150, they introduce us to two of the most feared lords of their day in Catalonia. Guilelm de Sant Martí was charged with "breaking into" the villages of Gavà, Sant Climent, and Viladecans ("Dogstown")—these are places of the Llobregat delta just west of Barcelona; he and his squires allegedly seized peasants' donkeys and grain and imposed labor services on them. At about the same time the people of Terrassa in the great valley north of the city complained to the Count about one Deusde (the name means "God-given") who, they said, seized from them and beat them. The names multiply with the charges: *Bernardus Mironis* and some ten other men and women at Gavà; *Petrus Guilelmi* of Brugera and his (unnamed) wife among some twenty-eight people who charged Deusde with violence at Terrassa.

Troublemakers, the afflicted, and their names: these are what the memorials have to relate. But something more can be shaken out of these two early ones. They begin to let on about the happenings that made them. The scribe at Gavà gives himself away: although he doesn't say so (because no formulary for scribes told him to), I can tell from the way he formed his letters that he was Ponç the Scribe, who certainly wrote a document connected with the same domain in 1144, and who was one of the busiest and most competent servants of Count Raimund Berenguer IV. The seizures in the Llobregat villages he wrote down seem to tell of two lordships in conflict, that of the Count being vulnerable to Guilelm de Sant Martí muscling in with his men to impose his own. The bailiffs and other servants charged together with Guilelm were surely known to Ponç the Scribe if not to those who complained; on the other side the Count's bailiff was said to have been ousted from a holding of land appointed to the Count's service. So what we have is an account, partly itemized, of a violated domain, written from the inside by a clerk conversant with the Lord-Count's interests in a prospering and visible locality.[8]

Terrassa's complaints figure even more vividly in a memorial carefully composed by a less expert scribe. He did, first of all in our series, what Ponç had not bothered to do: he said explicitly that the people of Terrassa were addressing their grievances to the Count of Barcelona. If the record of seizures at Gavà was likewise produced for the Count, it begins to look as if the latter had ordered an inquiry into conditions in his domains. The troubles at Terrassa

8. On the Llobregat domains see generally *FAC*, i, 169–170, 172; ii, no. 1CD; on Ponç the Scribe (d. 1168), i, 65–66, 246–247; ii, nos. 140, 1C.

were ascribed only to Deusde, which may only mean that this scribe was less informed than Ponç about accomplices. Deusde, a member of the Cardona family of barons, had been castellan at Terrassa since 1130 on condition of faithful service to the counts of Barcelona. His commended lordship, somewhat like that of Guilelm in the Llobregat vills, encroached on the Count's right to peasants' services and dues, which must have seemed to him a natural protectorate, his own for the taking.[9] We read of this in words of regularity and emotional restraint. The record refers to "head-cracking" (*fregit caput*) with breathtaking equanimity. But it also suggests that the memorializing of complaint was a subjective exercise in which the scribe might become actor as well as intermediary. The anonymous writer at Terrassa seems a little less suppressive than Ponç in the Llobregat places, yet there is nothing to help us understand how the "people of Terrassa" told of their grievances, nor even whether the suffering and telling drew them together.

How much more expressive a scribe could be becomes evident in our next memorial, which dates from about 1150 and takes us some fifty miles northeast of Barcelona. It presents itself as a *capbreu* of complaint: "This is a brief of many evil deeds which Arnal de Perella did and does to the Lord Count and his peasants." Far longer than its companion pieces, this record was written in sixty-five lines in a single skilled hand on a large piece of parchment; and it continues for ten additional lines on the reverse. What it says is that one Arnal de Perella and his cronies have mistreated the peasants at Caldes de Malavella and Llagostera, two villages south of Girona. And it says so in a uniquely informative manner. It begins with an extended narrative account of Arnal's misdeeds. The substance of this, which is too long to paraphrase here, will be of great interest in its place. All I need to observe here is that it describes an

9. On Terrassa and Deusde, *FAC*, i, 171–172; ii, no. 1Q.

allegedly arrogant master of equivocal status making uncustomary demands on peasants, neglecting his own obligations in comital service, living a lordly life of conspicuous consumption, usurping judicial payments, driving out bailiffs, and creating his own faction of favored men to the "great injury" of the Count and his people.

Following this narration, which takes up a third of the text, the scribe left two lined spaces blank, then continued with a short section detailing value or money taken from individual peasants since the Count's campaign against the Muslims of Almería (1147). Then comes another long paragraph specifying seizures and forced payments of many kinds from no fewer than eighty-two persons: men, women and clerics. The interest of this section, as will appear, is to show how justice could be exploited. The section ends by specifying that the foregoing "account of money" pertains to Caldes de Malavella. There follows a "brief of the bailiwick of Llagostera": specified loans not repaid, judicial payments, extortions from people "whom he threw out of the vill of Llagostera." This part continues on the reverse of the parchment, leading without further break to the mention of an occasion when Arnal de Perella "came to Caldes and Llagostera" and made yet more demands in payments and unpaid loans.

No such summation can do justice to this memorial. It is the single greatest record of its kind from Catalonia's twelfth century. I shall engage with it in later chapters, without much hope of unlocking all its secrets. Considered simply as a piece of medieval writing, it is an astonishing performance. A scribe (once again unnamed), whether in the distracting presence of his informants or from memory, appears to have comprehended specific allegations in a historical narration of considerable power. This need not have been beyond the ability of a local cleric, but a more likely explanation may be that some peasant or priest of these localities served as informant or author, the scribe taking his dictation. A good candidate for such a role would be one *Arnallus Granelli,* who was bailiff of Caldes in 1151 and who was described wryly in the memorial as having once been "rich and is now poor." He would have had some record of peasant losses at the hands of their vicar while having grievances of his own. He would have welcomed the invitation to let the Count know how his lordship was being exercised in these prospering domains. The unruffled regularity of the writing strongly suggests that the memorial as we have it represents a distillation of multiple testimonies from people who were visited or convoked for the purpose. Whatever the ways of indignant recollection, the accounting assumed a moral veneer more pronounced than in any of the memorials yet introduced. That, too, may be a sign that written memory in this record has been placed at one remove from the voices of complaint. Arnal de Perella is not merely charged, he is stigmatized. Yet as other records show, his position was not exactly the same as those of Guilelm de Sant Martí and Deusde in their places, nor were the charges against Arnal the same. He was not a castellan, but a vicar—that is, someone officially engaged in the Count's justice—and that, as we shall see, made a difference.[10]

The habitual absence of a Lord-Count preoccupied by enterprises on the Moorish frontier and in Provence helps to explain the grievances of Caldes and Llagostera. In Llagostera the bailiffs were *Berengarius Mironis* and *Petrus Tosa* when the domain was surveyed in 1151. Their work—or at any rate, their offers—continued to satisfy the Count's chief accountant, for the same two men repurchased the right to collect revenues in the comital bailiwick of Llagostera in 1160. And it happens that a third man of that place— his name was *Guilelmus Ponci*—had an interest in the work of those bailiffs, for he not only swore to the accuracy of the survey by order of the bailiffs *Berengarius* and *Petrus* in 1151, he also attended the sale of the bailiwick to the same two men in 1160. He, for one, surely knew what was going on in the fields of Llagostera! So it is startling

---

10. On Caldes de Malavella and Llagostera, *FAC,* i, 174–176; ii, no. 1GH; on Arnal de Perella, also ii, no. 4 (ll. 24, 62); i, 25, 51–52, 68, 71–76, 251.

to find *Guilelmus Ponci* himself attesting the truth of complaints against the same *Berengarius Mironis* in a "commemoration of misdeeds" at some time uncertain during these years.

This event figures in a small parchment bearing three series of allegations, two in one continuous hand, the third added in a second hand. Here again the opening is explicit: "This is a commemoration of misdeeds which Ber. Mir is doing unjustly to his lord R. Berenguer Count of Barcelona and Prince of Aragon." So it becomes ever clearer that the Lord-Count was expressly concerned about the deportment of his servants in his domains; and it begins to look as if some formulary of inquiry, or questionnaire, had been imposed: namely, what injuries to the Lord-Count of Barcelona (that is, to his lordship) have been suffered? And in this case the allegations are comparable to those against Arnal de Perella. Berenguer Mir (for so I shall now call him) was said to have encroached on the Count's lordship in the honors or vills of Esclet and Ganix, depriving the Count of agrarian dues and impositions. At Cabanyes he had seized the vineyard of a departed tenant, accepted a half-manse in gift without paying tallage or providing services, and developed new agrarian lordships while "the Count lost his tasc and tithe. And *Guilelmus Ponci* knows that what is written here is true."

So this memorial concludes, uniquely, with its proof of authorship. "And *Guilelmus Ponci* knows. . . ." It looks as if he himself was the informant and that the scribe wished to disclaim responsibility by naming him. Which is, after all, what might be expected in villages where the allegations exposed not so much violations as usurpations, where the violator, comfortably in office, might expect to escape denunciation. For all its seeming innocence, this record evokes an obscure hinterland of stress as do few of the others. And, here as at Caldes, it was hard to recount misfortunes without telling stories. Did it matter that the former tenant at Cabanyes had gone to Tarragona? Yes, because one remembered that he had possessed a "good big vineyard" free of the impositions

Berenguer Mir had lately imposed. To account was to remember; the writing of specific account was a new story in its laconic and economical way; but the *petite histoire* which first came with it might leave its trace, an undissolved residue of explanation.[11]

If a scribe could convey one man's complaints objectively, so could he represent multiple complaints subjectively. This is what happened at Font-rubí, a village in the region of Penedès some thirty miles west of Barcelona, in the 1150s. Here indeed, for the first time, we meet a community speaking through its scribe, and what is more, again for the first time, doing so repeatedly. It is true that in a second memorial, dating from 1162–1165, another scribe reverted to the more normal third-person form of discourse, but in yet a third record from Font-rubí dating from perhaps a year or two later the voiced "we" of the community is once again immediate. These memorials form a uniquely sustained testimony in our series, nor are they all of their kind that survive from Font-rubí.

The first of these pieces may seem the work of a not very literate scribe. His Latin is poorly inflected, like that of his fellow at Terrassa; his spoken vernacular pokes through repeatedly. But illiteracy is the wrong charge. His lettering is all but faultless in a sure and practised hand. Items are set off by points and capital letters. It is only that the scribe is so caught up himself in the vernacular expression he shares and conveys that the artifice of his latinity sags. Yet with near perfect consistency he succeeds in preserving the plural "we" and "us" in complaints addressed to "the Count who is our best Lord." Moreover, the people of Font-rubí address their Lord-Count personally, and they do so with passion, pleading for redress of grievances, "for your mercy." Only in the beginning, where the Count himself is charged with having imposed taxes "on us which we never had in the life of his father [*suum pater,* sic]," does the

---

11. On Esclet, Ganix, Berenguer Mir, and Guilelm Ponç, *FAC,* i, 73–74, 175–176; ii, nos. 14, 10,E.

scribe lurch into a clumsily descriptive mode. For the rest he iden-
tifies with the community, telling the Lord-Count how his vicars
have imposed "great forces and tolts on us," specifying seizures of
barley and wheat from individuals by the Lady of Mediona, by
Raimund de Barbera, by Berenguer de Bleda, and by their men.

The writing fills an amply cut parchment comparable to the one
from Caldes and Llagostera. It ends with a ringing apostrophe to
Count Raimund, having quite the appearance of finality. But then
it refuses to stop talking. On the reverse appears what looks like a
continuation of the record, in writing so badly effaced that I cannot
be sure it is the same scribe's work, let alone read it. Below this,
headed by the words "Complaints of the men of Font-rubí," were
written thirty-one further lines in a different script dating perhaps
from a few years later. Of this distinct text, enough can be read to
show that it is, or was, a complete memorial of further complaints
against Berenguer de Bleda; not enough to earn it a numbered
place in my assemblage of witnesses. Clinging to its elder sibling,
rare evidence of the subsequent handling of these parchments, it is
one of a series of four survivors from its locality, quite possibly
subsequent to one or both of the pieces next in order.[12]

The two subsequent records from Font-rubí have the formality
of routine. Both begin with declarations that the people of this
castle-vill are complaining about Berenguer de Bleda and his castellans. Both name people, offenders as well as victims, but not many,
preferring to generalize about an experience represented as associative. As a result the people who *are* named—such as the lady castellan Berengaria de Puigdàlber, said to have broken into *Carbo's*
house, and *Martinus de Fonterubeo,* whose tale of eviction is of arresting interest—are something more than mere items at Font-rubí.
Like the longer early memorial, that of c. 1162–1165 is of special
value for what it says of the tormentors' pretensions. The representation of complaint is less personally involved, telling objec-

12. On Font-rubí, *FAC,* i, 207–208; *CC,* iii, 642–643.

tively that "they" or "he" complain(s); yet once again subjective feeling breaks through. At the end the grievances are addressed affectively to the Lord-King (Alfons I, 1162–1196), in phrases both familiar (*tibi*) and formal (*vobis*).[13]

The final memorial in this series makes no such subjective appeal to the Lord-King. Moreover, save on one conspicuous point—the pulling of "our beards," which is also attested in the first memorial—the particulars are different, relating chiefly to forced services and the driving of domestic animals to Barcelona and elsewhere. Yet here too the modes of discourse vacillate, moving from descriptive third-person declarations to affective representations in which the scribe seems to share in the lamentation. Indeed, more than most, this scribe conveys something of the cadence of collective complaint: so for example, in the old days "we held our manses" for a single sheaf of feedgrain, "and now today" for three or four. Still, there is less passion here than in the appeal to Count Raimund, with which it shares a characteristic concern with honor.[14]

Two further memorials give voice to the heartlands of the old county of Barcelona. The first describes itself as a "commemoration of the land of Valmala which Dorca holds." A record of rural tenures and obligations held from and owed to the Count of Barcelona, it appears to date from the later years of Raimund Berenguer IV. Then from the years after 1162 comes a record of troubles at Lower Corró (Corró d'Avall), some twenty miles northeast of Barcelona, a record as vividly transparent as that of Valmala is inscrutable.

For it is not easy to decide what Valmala's scribe thought he was doing. If his first words hardly respond to the directive perceptible in other memorials, the gist of his account is rather like them. The

13. See note 12.
14. See note 12.

tenures were organized as a benefice in the hands of Dorca, who is then listed himself among some thirty-four men who had fields in several places, including *Pegeres, Manleu, Sant Llorenç,* and *Canoves.* These places are the key to another little mystery: the location of the "land of Valmala." The only place where they can be found clustered is Osona, the space of an old county absorbed by Barcelona in the eleventh century. And as it happens, a charter of the year 936 refers to a *Vallmala* ("Bad Valley") located in Osona in easy proximity to Manlleu, Canoves, and Sant Llorenç; so I think it a likely conjecture that Valmala was indeed a "land" of dispersed comital tenancies loosely adjoining those of the eastern Vallès, including Corró, to the south. Probably the only domain in Osona retained by the twelfth-century counts, it would have been held by Dorca on terms like those of Deusde at Terrassa or Arnal at Caldes de Malavella.[15]

So much from a small parchment fluently inscribed in ill-inflected Latin. Yet, it clings to its secrets. Who wrote it, and why? It begins (and ends) like a *capbreu,* in descriptively normative discourse. Only once does the scribe represent words personally: "I *Pelegrino* [hold] one field at *Ermengarda* and we give tasc." Was this simply a lapse betraying the voiced words of the (anonymous) scribe's informants? Or could it be that *Pelegrinus* himself wrote the memorial, recording himself among other tenants? Either way it looks as if someone wished the Count to know of shortcomings in the service of his tenants. The first entries, for Dorca himself and for four other tenants (including a woman, *Ermessen*), appear to

15. The charter is printed in *Diplomatari de la catedral de Vic, segles IX–X,* ed. Eduard Junyent i Subirà. Patronat d'Estudis ausonencs (Vic, 1980), no. 364. It was drawn to my attention by my friends Mn. Dr. Miquel S. Gros and Dra. Immaculada Ollich, whom I thank warmly. *Vallis mala* is also attested in *Catalunya carolíngia,* ed. Ramon d'Abadal i de Vinyals, 3 vols. to date (Barcelona, 1926–86), ii[1], 173, a diploma for Ripoll of 982. A place named *Canovès* is attested in the parish of Sant Julià de Vilatorta, Arxiu Capitular de Vic, calaix 6, 1070 (3 vi 1080).

represent them as withholding renders from the Count (or possibly as seizing them from other tenants at the Count's expense). Thereafter the verb *tollere* (to take) is replaced by *donare* (to give, render) so as to make clear that most tenancies benefit the Count. One further detail supports this reading. When Dorca's tenure of a field at *Pegeres* is mentioned, it is added that "he gives nothing" for it. The same is recorded of four other tenants. Is there not here too, as at Terrats and elsewhere, something between the lines?

At Corró the obscurity lifts. Four men together with "all other enfranchised men who are his own your men [sic] complain to you our Lord King [Alfons I] about Pere de Bell-lloc who broke into your village of Corró and often dragged out your men bound by the throat and put them in prison and perpetrated many misdeeds which he cannot say to you, Lord, in writing. First, he took from me, *Pages,* fourteen sheep and seventeen geese and one cape and deprived me of my harvests. And from me *Arnallus de Valoria* he broke into my manse and made such a ruckus that I cannot live there. . . ." And so on. Here we are close to the lamentation. No protocol intrudes to organize plaintiffs and their writer, who, like Ponç the Scribe at Gavà, seems merely to have asked: "What happened?" But here for the first time I hear the villagers themselves speaking through the record, first as the community of free men (*franchearii*) they claimed to be, then as the Lord-Count's tenants seriatim. It appears from telling details that the writer's decision to preserve the individual voices was conscious and problematic. In the first lines he wrote: "we complain to our Lord-King," then added (following "complain"): "to you"; and he then wrote: "[we free men] who are his own men" before adding: "your [*uestri*]." It is likely that the first correction, perhaps with villagers looking over his shoulders, was made at once, for the second correction betrays no hesitation or second thought. These may seem ephemeral details. Yet they are not useless, for they help me to glimpse a human scene in its cultural-institutional ambivalence: some villagers and their scribe reserving the subjective orality of lordship against the encroachment of written official action.[16]

This ambivalence shows up even more strikingly in two memorials of complaint from the Ribes valley bordering Cerdanya. Dating from a time between the accession of Alfons I in 1162 and about 1170, these are so nearly alike in form and scripts that I suppose them to be the work of a single scribe. Depositions from peasants at Ribes and Pardines were put down in writing which neatly fills a strip of parchment, others from Queralbs on a second, smaller piece, again with no space to spare. It is of interest that in this land of sheep the second memorial was written on a membrane apparently cut from an evangeliary, as if the gathering of depositions had imposed an unexpected strain on the supplies of local scribes. Both records conclude with declarations of truth in the intention of placing the charges before the King's court; the memorial of Ribes adds: "in his court according to his directive," thus making fully explicit the purpose of these inquiries. The object of these charges, all of them, was a castellan named Raimund de Ribes, who held judicial powers in the Ribes valley. The villagers accused him of seizing money and property and of constraining them to pay fines on any excuse or on none at all. "R. de Ribes took away from *Guilelmus Iozbert* 7[s.] for a certain boy, his brother, who had died." "R. de Ribes took away from me *Petrus Arnad* one excellent cow, I don't know why." Some forty-eight peasants recounted their injuries at the hands of a local tyrant who seems to have placed intimidation at the service of greed.

On first sight one might read these memorials as a continuous

16. Corró was an extended hill vill, with settlements above (*d'Amunt*) and below (*d'Avall*). The memorial almost certainly relates to Corró d'Avall, which would have been the more vulnerable to external attack. The manse of Valoria figures in a *capbreu* for Corró d'Avall dating from the time of R.B. IV, and so does *Guilelmus Guitardi*'s manse, *FAC*, ii, no. 14; see also i, 30, 32, 40, 100n91, 168–169.

record, so similar are they in substance and appearance. But the scribe not only completed each piece with a closing declaration, he (if it was indeed one person) did something else to distinguish between his own works of representation. He put down the complaints of Ribes in objective, third-person discourse, and those of Queralbs in the subjective voices of the peasants themselves. The difference is illustrated by the items quoted above, which are typical, and it is observed almost absolutely. It may seem idle to insist on this divergence of perspective: both memorials efficiently represent the very words of the peasants. Yet it matters that the scribe's relation to peasants crowded about him changed from one record to the other, for here again a resonant echo of perplexity seems to betray the ambiguity of social identity. Whether the scribe changed his mind overnight or came progressively to decide on a subjective representation of complaint (for that seems, indeed, to have been the order of composition) can only be guessed, but it was manifestly a conscious change. These are the two most consistently and economically worded memorials of our whole set.[17]

From the years around 1160 comes a long memorial of complaints by the lord Guilelm de Castellvell against his castellan Berenguer. The "old castle" where their power was centered lay on the old frontier just west of the Llobregat River some fifteen miles northwest of Barcelona. It was already a great lordship in Guilelm's day, one which was vulnerable to encroachments by an ambitious vassal-servant who shared in its proceeds. The burden of the grievance is that Berenguer has usurped lordly powers, imposed uncustomary taxes, and constrained people to the point of capricious violence. He has thrown people in prison, cut off a woman's nose, and threatened to blind peasants or cut off their feet. Much else is detailed in charges which fill a spacious parchment in crowded lines

17. On the Ribes valley, *FAC*, i, 185–186; ii, nos. 7, 15, 53, 55, 131; on Raimund de Ribes, i, 185, 275; ii, no. 7. The folio that became ACA, Cancelleria, perg. extrainv. 3217 bears a reading from Matthew 10.18.

of tolerably correct Latin. There is no problem of perspective here. The complaints are represented objectively as Guilelm wished them to be heard, doubtless in a royal court (for only so would the memorial have found a place in the Lord-King's archives).

Strictly speaking, this memorial is an interloper in my select array. It is not directly concerned with peasant grievances, belonging rather to a distinct class of complaints deployed by barons in their suits against one another. Guilelm's memorial is indeed a rarely engaging example of this genre, filled with illuminating details about a great lord's expectations of commended servants. Moreover, there survives an equally informative list of Berenguer's complaints against Guilelm de Castellvell, possibly prepared for the same tribunal. But let us not be distracted. Guilelm's memorial, and his alone, contains evidence of the treatment of peasants that is not only inherently plausible but also tends to bear out records of rural grievances elsewhere. This piece has a pertinence and steady clarity that will prove welcome.[18]

Yet another oddity survives to throw light on troubles in the King's domains, this time at a place on the new frontier not far from the Cistercian houses of Poblet and Santes Creus. It is a complaint from the years c. 1173–1175 by a royal bailiff (or former bailiff) named Bertran de Vilafranca addressed in passionately personal terms to the Lord-King Alfons; and here again we have also what look like counter-allegations by two of the individuals charged by Bertran. Even so, these records are so different in form and appearance that I must describe them separately, which means to risk getting them the wrong way round. If I call first on Bertran's memorial, it is

18. See generally Bonaventura Pedemonte i Falguera, *Notes per a la història de la Baronia de Castellvell de Rosanes* . . . (Barcelona, 1929), pp. 105–120; Blanca Garí, *El linaje de los Castellvell en los siglos XI y XII.* Medievalia, monografias 5 (Bellaterra, 1985), part III, esp. pp. 153, 170–177; and idem, "Las *querimoniae* feudales," 10–18.

chiefly because I find it harder to imagine his adversaries getting up *their* charges unprovoked.[19]

Bertran's memorial, I say, because here for once the text reads like a personal letter. Bertran, layman though he undoubtedly was, may even have written it. He refers to the violent seizure of lands at Cabra "during eight years when I Bertran de Vilafranca was bailiff . . . And know, my royal Lord, that I Bertran de Vilafranca" am reviled because of your commands which I imposed. Even if a scribe wrote from Bertran's dictation, the words preserved are as close to spoken Catalan as anything to be found in the memorials of complaint. Bertran's narration touches on abuses diversely; it seems hurried, almost breathless. What lends unity to his charges is his aggrieved sense that his Lord-King's trust has been violated. Berenguer de Clariana has seized money, property, and the King's share of wine from "your man" *Poncius de Barbera*. He has taken money from "your man" *Berengarius de Pugol*, and so on. The weightiest allegations are that Berenguer and his knights have pillaged "your palace" at Cabra and have appropriated royal domains; "and the men of Cabra dare not appeal to you for fear of those knights, for you are far off and they are near us." Berenguer and his knights have so oppressed the people with "forces, tolts, and quests" that "everyone went away, they with their possessions, to other places." Spontaneously Bertran associates himself with the villagers in these grievances, yet his impulse seems as much personal as official.

The same remark may be made in reverse about the charges levelled *against* Bertran de Vilafranca by the very men he had accused (if, to repeat, I have the order right). But in this memorial Guilelm de Concabella and Berenguer de Clariana have the temerity to list the "good men of Cabra" together with themselves as the very authors of complaints here set out as regularly and carefully as

19. There may be a better reason: if *A. de Muntfred* was ransomed (Ca1-2609), it probably happened before he was dispossessed (Ca2-3474).

Bertran's effort was untidy. They have enlisted an expert scribe whose Latin is well-nigh faultless. Running out of space on a small parchment irregularly cut, he continued the narration to its summary conclusion on the reverse.

The charges are that Bertran has dispossessed people from their holdings, imprisoned them, and harassed them "by many evil deeds" to the point of driving them away from Cabra. He seized, ransomed, and sold what he took from *Arnaldus de Monte frigido* (or *Muntfred*, "Cold Mount") to the monks at Santes Creus for 400s. "without the King's license or ours." *Arnal de Muntfred* figures also in Bertran's memorial, less as offender than victim in a passage admittedly murky, which may be one reason for believing that Bertran's memorial came first. But the charges against Bertran in no way respond to his own. They represent him, not implausibly, as a heavy-handed lord (he is not called bailiff), with no better claim to local power than their own. *Arnallus de Valle spinosa* for one seems to have had grievances against both contending appellants, a predicament doubtless shared by many at Cabra. But the second scribe kept his distance, with perhaps only the word "ours" (*nostra*, quoted above) hinting at his sympathy for the associative intent of his authors. Nor does his representation underscore the King's losses, as elsewhere, or the failings of official action in his service. Bertran de Vilafranca is revealed in this complementary perspective as one of several local lords with conflicting stakes at Cabra. That he spoke up for himself gives his accusers' memorial much of its interest.[20]

My final and latest witness (c. 1180–1190) is a memorial of "complaints which the people of Argençola make to the Lord God and to my King of all their goods which Berenguer de Clariana and his men unjustly took away from them. First," it says, "*A. Barba rossa* ["Red-beard"] lost 13 mitgers of barley 3 mitgers of wheat 5 quar-

---

20. On Cabra del Camp and Bertran de Vilafranca, *FAC*, i, 214, 216, 264.

ters of farina . . .," some towels worth 3s., clothing, meat, live pigs, chickens, honey, "and very many other things which he can't remember." Then came losses itemized by *P. Barbarossa, Berengarius de Vilanova, Perdigo,* and others to a total of twelve persons whose detailed claims cover the face of a rather large parchment. As he ran out of space, the scribe noted that his record was incomplete, omitting the malefactions suffered by Berenguer de Aguiló and his knights. Continuing on the reverse, this notation refers to the burning of their lord Berenguer's castle, apparently that of Argençola, reckons total losses at Argençola at ten thousand sous' worth, and envisages a hearing in the Lord-King's court.

This memorial is hardly other than an inventory of losses in a form imposed by the scribe. One by one he wrote up their claims, starting with grain and wine, then listing other items of property. Having begun in long lines, he divided his space into columns for the third and subsequent depositions, neatly marking off each person's claims by horizontal lines. The language is an incorrect but fluent Latin governed entry by entry by the verb *perdidit* ("so and so lost"), but with the items mostly in the vernacular. And while losses are represented objectively, it becomes clear at the end that the scribe was imposing his order on a subjective consensus. This revelation may have resulted from running out of space; but in any case the writer could not fully record *Beregarius Maria,* because by reason of his losses he had left his family and gone away, "and we don't know where he lives." Three others also lost property and went away, producing a helpless affirmation that wherever they are they have lost everything.

So the underlying sense of shared grievance breaks through the written formality. The "men of Argençola" spoke, yet they were only twelve; and at least eleven of them had got through the ordeal. They continued to reside in their village, they hoped for redress. Whether by their restraint or by the scribe's preference—or perhaps now by the King's wish?—their record was not to be a history or a lamentation, but an accounting; a memorial not so much of trouble as of its consequences. "Berenguer de Clariana and his men," "Berenguer de Aguiló and his knights": little enough is left to be imagined. But only the former were charged. Berenguer de Aguiló seems to have shared in the villagers' ordeal, which may have been in some part an incident of warfare between the Berenguers. The former was surely the same lord who had been accused at Cabra, twenty kilometers to the south; Berenguer of Aguiló bore the name of a castle between Argençola and Cabra. But their violence as such, so visible in the memorials of Gavà, Corró, and Cabra, is of small interest in this memorial.[21]

There they are, these parchments, these sixteen (more or less) vestiges of inquiries into the conditions of peasants who lived long ago. They come from every part of Catalonia where the counts of Barcelona had direct lordship. *Pere Oler* lived at Argençola, *Maienca* at Llagostera, *Petrus Faber* at Ribes. Did the Count-Prince's peasants know their grievances were so widely shared? It seems unlikely, for not even their scribes saw clear of the peculiarities of local circumstance. Little but the framing verbiage of fragmentary protocols in several of the pieces survives to prove an impulse of sovereign justice. The memorials do not so much represent local interactions or interrogations as remember them. Scribes wrote on whatever parchments they found to hand, some of them too small for their present need. They wrote in a colloquial Latin shot through with spoken Catalan. They found themselves, or placed themselves, diversely in relation to the voiced allegations, in a spectrum ranging from objective recording to subjective engagement.

And the scribes functioned, more or less officially, with sublime (or canny?) disregard for their own role. Constrained by no notarial form to identify themselves, preoccupied by an oppressive present,

21. On Argençola, *CC*, v, 161–164; *Catalunya romànica*, ed. Joan Ainaud i de Lasarte, Antoni Pladevall et al., 23 vols. (Barcelona: Encìclopedia Catalona, 1984– [in progress]), xix (1992), 365–366. When referring hereafter to *Beregarius Maria*, I shall silently restore the "n" omitted by the scribe: *Bere[n]garius*.

they produced records careless of posterity. Only one of their memorials—the recognition for Terrats which, cut off from its lawful
mate, was manifestly intended to prove lawful right—bears any
formal sign of interest in a terrestrial future. Yet they stop their
moments for us, these moral photographs, inviting us to pore over
them. Won't they yield something more than details to *our* interest
in these forgotten moments of truth? It is the people they name,
not the records, who struggle on in ways forever lost to sight, yet
forever potent in the images of discontent left on parchment. *Iohanes Macíp's* wife. *Martin de Riu. Raimundus Marti.* . . .

[II]

PEOPLE

It is not easy to represent them collectively. Plaintiffs, accused, subjects of inert or inept description, these people do not speak for a society. They speak—or rather, with few exceptions, are made to speak—for themselves. I can count them, can name them, can reflect on the meaning of some details of their standing and associations, but I can *not* surely say what proportion of the villagers or peasants protested. At Caldes de Malavella some ninety-one persons (or households) are mentioned, a fact that compares so well with the 115 manses recorded in a fiscal survey of 1151 that I feel justified in supposing that virtually the whole village claimed abuse by Arnal de Perella. On the other hand, only eleven persons claimed injury at Gavà, Viladecans, and Sant Climent, which can hardly have amounted to all the settlers in those burgeoning places. Moreover, the records of their witness are separated in time by intervals up to fifty years—that is, in one or two cases at least, by more than a generation. Even the contemporary plaintiffs at Gavà, Terrassa, and Caldes/Llagostera, or, a little later, at Font-rubí and Ribes, can hardly have known each other in rural habitats disparately and distantly clustered. Still another difficulty attaches to social status. It may be tempting but is certainly misleading to suppose that the memorials refer to a mass of peasants exploited by a few local bullies of commonly elite status. For beneath that appearance lay diverse social realities that defy easy equations, divergencies of wealth and status within or between regions. These long forgotten people may be deemed typical of their populations, but they cannot be treated as a collectivity, still less as a community.[1]

The memorials refer to upwards of five hundred people. I cannot be more precise than this, for two reasons: first, because it is not always clear whether a repeated given name refers to the same or to a second (or third) person; and second, because there are allusions to persons unnamed in the plural, such as to squires (*armigeri*) and knights (*homines*) who were said to have perpetrated violence at Gavà, Font-rubí, and Cabra. According to testimony at Caldes de Malavella there used to be "a hundred young men" who had money and grain, "and now not a single one is there." But plenty of others were still there and elsewhere. In some fifteen villages or domains 305 men and seven women are named as injured or making deposition or as involved with the plaintiffs together with at least thirty-five alleged tormentors, including four women. In addition figure men and women unnamed: kinsfolk (wives, husbands, sons, daughters, even a stepdaughter), neighbors and malefactors, as well as bailiffs, millers, priests, monks, and others identified by function, for a total of more than one hundred further individuals. These allusions add up to some 449 people, of whom 347 (77 percent), are known to us by given names. And from these names may be glimpsed one larger facet of an aggregate population.[2]

1. *FAC*, ii, no. 1G; C-Ll-2501, G3451, F1–3 (3409, 3141, 3288), R1–2 (3433, 3217).

2. Observations based on all the memorials of complaint. As signalled in Chapter I, note 1, I shall not always hereafter cite the sixteen selected memorials for places and familiar names mentioned in the text. They can be identified (if desired) from the list in Appendix 4.

These are Mediterranean people. Their parents named their sons Pere (Peter) more often than any other, a preference then becoming common everywhere in the Christian West; but they also named them Arnal, Berengar, Bernard, Guilelm, Johan, Ponç, and Raimund. The clustering of these favored masculine names, together with Ermengarda and Ermessen for the women, locates this population within a south Frankish zone extending from the Ebro River northeastward across the Pyrenees to Provence. To judge from excellent recent studies of naming patterns in Occitania, some tendencies visible in our sample were characteristic of this whole Mediterranean region. Peasant men and women received and bestowed the same names as the knights, lords and ladies who dominated them. Except for Pere, a name borne by no fewer than seventy-one of male subjects in the Catalonian memorials (or 21 percent), preferred names continued to be Germanic rather than Roman or Christian, with Guilelm (11 percent) and Raimund (9 percent) in the lead. It is true that Johan and Ponç figure (with Pere) among the eight most popular names, yet even taken together they account for only 6 percent of the total, while the Christian names *Deusdedit, Maria,* and *Martinus* are altogether rare. As in Occitania female names remain many and diverse, with all but two of eleven women bearing a different name; while the more numerous but less varied list of fifty-eight masculine names (in a sample of 335) has the appearance of reduction from a once much larger pool to a favored repertory of about fifteen names. Again as beyond the Pyrenees and indeed everywhere else, the Catalonian memorials show that in the twelfth century scribes were feeling the need, even when dealing with peasants, to distinguish one *Petrus* or *Guilelmus* from another. Only fifty-one of these people (or 14.7 percent), bear unqualified names like Ademar, Geralla, or Vital. Some 40 percent of our male population was recorded with compound names in apparently familial or patronymic forms, such as *Petrus Dalmatii* or *Raimundus Sunier.* Toponymic surnames—as in *Berengarius de Soler, Poncius de Barbera*—account for another 27 percent; which leaves a residue of about forty-four compound names (13 percent) with appellatives that resist easy categorizing.[3]

All these features have a broadly Mediterranean appearance. While the choice of Pere or Johan drew on currents of reformed Christianity, the names Guilelm and Raimund, likewise baptismal, resonated with venerable traditions of anti-Moorish sovereign power. By the middle of the twelfth century public memories of heroic conflict had dimmed, leaving only a vague sense of security in choosing prestigious names. But there are also singularities to mark off my sample as Catalan. Berengar and Iohan take the places of Bertran and Huc amongst favored names. Ermengarda, Ermessen, and Maienca, which account for five of the eleven named women, were notably typical of Catalonia. And there was a tendency for the appellatives in compound names to assume distinctively vernacular forms, whether as occupational attributes or as patronymics: for example, *Arnad torner, Dominicus Roi, P. Bou, Pere rossel.* Whether the naming patterns point to localisms within Catalan-speaking lands is harder to say. The nomenclature at Terrats has a slightly archaic aspect, with its several single names, including Oliba. This is the only occurrence of that venerable Pyrenean appellation as a given name in the entire documentation. Yet this memorial also registers, for the nine names attaching to eleven men, no fewer than five of the most widely popular names: Arnald, Berengar, Pere, Raimund, and Wilelm (Guilelm). In subsequent memorials I can see that toponymics tend to reflect local realities— for example, *Berengarius de Bleta, Carbo de Fonte rubeo,* and *Dominicus Moix de Penedès* (referring respectively to castles in the Penedès

3. See generally Jean-Louis Biget, "L'évolution des noms de baptême en Languedoc au moyen-âge (IXe–XIVe s.)," *Liturgie et musique (IXe–XIVe s.).* Cahiers de Fanjeaux 17 (Fanjeaux, 1982), pp. 297–341; Monique Bourin, "Les formes anthroponymiques et leur évolution d'après les données du cartulaire du chapitre cathédral d'Agde (Xe siècle–1250)," *Genèse médiévale de l'anthroponymie moderne,* 3 vols. (5 parts). Etudes d'anthroponymie médiévale (Tours, 1989–95), i, 179–217. Also Enric Bagué, *Noms personals de l'edat mitjana. Contribució a la història cultural dels Països Catalans* (Palma de Mallorca, 1975).

and to a vill near Llagostera)—but no argument can be founded
on common sense like this. The prevailing anthroponymy points
to a cultural identity still broadly west Mediterranean as well as
Catalan.[4]

The people who inhabit the memorials once lived in the countrysides. All of them. Even the alleged malefactors, even the nameless and uncounted horsemen, squires, bailiffs, and clerics in the
vague mentions of whom the scribes could relax. Not one "city-
zen" is noted, no one from the bishops' towns of Barcelona, Girona, or Vic. *Adalyde of Perpignan* figures among the peasants at
Caldes de Malavella and she may possibly have come from her
name's place northward across the mountains one could see from
Caldes. But Perpignan was little more than a village in her day, at
most a way station for the Count's entourage, knights, and mer-
chants. The scribes were in no doubt that the people to whom they
gave ear were collectively peasants: *pagenses* at Gavà and Sant Climent in the Llobregat delta and also at Caldes and Llagostera,
"rustics" (*rustici*) there and in the Ribes valley. These terms would
have been understood also in those villages, such as Font-rubí and
Cabra, where the scribes tended to identify psychologically with
their subjects. They were socially descriptive terms, not legal ones.
So was the word *homines,* which referred not only to commended
knights, but also diversely to the Count's peasant tenants and to
people of localities: thus, "people" (*homines*) at Font-rubí, of Queralbs, of Cabra, of Argençola. In two places the scribes gave added
precision to such mentions, designating the people of Corró as
"enfranchised men" (*franchearii*) and those of Cabra as "good men"
(*probi homines*). Both terms raise questions that will be of further
interest; what is clear at once is that in at least two places people
were conscious of an associative status setting off some from a mass
of individuals. The most cryptic social precision is to be found in
the lamentation that "masters and bachelors" were among the pros-

4. In addition to studies cited in note 3, see the index to *HL,* v.

perous young people who had fled Caldes and Llagostera. These terms appear to refer respectively to notables (or owners of property) and to aspirants to honorable service or knighthood.[5] There would have been such in every considerable village. Apart from these instances, the memorials betray difficulty in expressing social diversity through limited and untechnical vocabulary.

Yet it was not for lack of effort to express status in names. I can be quite sure that *Felix rusticus* and a "certain *rusticus Iohanes Oliba*," both of the upland village of Pardines, were regarded as country-dwellers; in no way sure how they differed from countless others not so designated. Was it perhaps that the scribe recorded them as he heard of them from others? "Rustic" described Felix without naming him. But it must have been otherwise with *Iohanes macíp* at Ribes and *Petrus mancip* at Caldes. Echoing an ancient slavery founded on possession (*mancipium*), these names remind us that John and Peter lived in venerable domains where slavery had disappeared only a few lifetimes before. The vernacular *mancip,* neither taint nor (probably) live memory, and perhaps by now meaning only "boy," was on its (Catalan) way to becoming a patronymic.[6] Other names seem less problematic. Because *A. Barba Rossa* (red beard) and *P. Barbarossa* were represented successively in the memorial for Argençola, I suppose that the appellative was a family name. On the other hand, the suffixes *testor* (read: *textor,* weaver) and *venditus-a* (literally, sold man or woman) in the record of Caldes-Llagostera certainly relate to occupation and status, as we shall see. And a world of works and days seems evoked in the names of Arnal the turner (*torner*), Pere *Pastorel,* Peter the worker (*faber*), and

5. C-Ll-2501: "et alios magistros et baculares. . . ." See translation below, p. 100; and *Glossarium mediae latinitatis Cataloniae . . .,* 9 fascicules to date (Barcelona, 1960–86), cols. 209–211 (s.v. *baccallarius*).

6. See Bonnassie, *La Catalogne,* i, 298–302; ii, 809–824. Cf. *Homilies d'Organyà. Edició facsímil del manuscrit núm. 289 de la Biblioteca de Catalunya,* ed. Joan Coromines (Barcelona, 1989), p. 50: "Quan om és macip, penssa aixi com macip e sab aixi com macip . . ." (interpreting 1 Cor. 13.11).

even *Guilelm* "hammer-head" (*caput mallei*). Ponç the clerk was not the only priest to suffer losses at Caldes and Llagostera, but few clergymen figure in the memorials.[7]

Everywhere people lived the experience of family and gender. The lordly entourages of Arnal de Perella and other vicars and castellans were only the most visible of characteristic families. Arnal's wife must have been a focal person in the *familia* that prospered in his power; she was said to have imposed herself like her husband, perhaps especially in his absence. The lady lord (*domna*) of Mediona was one of several women lords charged, like the male lords in my sample, with oppressive violence.[8] Most people of all estates lived in families headed by men. Most who complained, indeed the vast majority, were males. But they spoke for and about kinsfolk male and female: about wives, husbands, daughters, sons, even little boys and girls or infants; about sisters and brothers; about uncles and aunts; about men and women beyond the circle of blood relations. Men visibly felt responsible for this extended interest. *Petrus faber* lost 6s. because his aunt's box of valuables had been in his possession when Raimund de Ribes asked to see it. Or were held responsible: *Felix* had two cows taken from him at Pardines because his brother's wife died sterile. And if *Guilelmus Gerouart's* mother had a tooth knocked out, was it not because she had resisted Deusde's thefts from her son and others at Terrassa?

Women living in domains west of the Llobregat seem to have been particularly vulnerable to disfiguring physical injury, to judge from the reports of outraged men there; but everywhere women's losses were deplored as afflictions borne by men and their families. There was no insistence on feminine frailty or incompetence. Itemized losses were recorded for numerous women at Caldes and Llagostera, some of whom must have spoken for themselves. Women expressly represented their husbands (or families) on occa-

7. C-Ll-2501: *Poncius* and *Bernardus Udalardi, clerici,* plus an unnamed *monachus;* F1-3409: *Giu clericus;* Cast3509: *monachus* of Sant Genis.
8. C-Ll-2501, F1-3409.

sion. "Raimund de Ribes took from me *Ermessen* and my husband *Esbaldíd* 5s. because our child-son died, no other cause." Widowed mothers figure enough in the depositions to make it likely that sons routinely defended dowered property. At Gavà *A. de Plano* and his mother were said to have lost their landed inheritance to the coercive force of Guilelm de Sant Martí. And when *Pere Mir* was robbed of two oxen and a sheep in Pardines "nothing remained to him and his mother."

Except their house? That is, if they had one. Many of these people must have lived in houses belonging to others. The domestic inheritance was as precious to Catalan peasants as was the *domus* in Montaillou a century later. Its customs and beliefs largely escape us, for the memorials of complaint are less garrulous than Jacques Fournier's register of inquisition.[9] The memorials refer to the house as a building—the Latin is *domus* or *casa* (*kasa*)—vulnerable to attack or sequestration. Pride of possession and fear attached to the house and its furnishing, which provide us with a measure, however imperfect, of wealth and status.

But the house was not the only element of rural property. It was part of a complex of organized and constructed space referred to as the manse (*mansus*) at Terrats, Corró, Castellvell, Caldes and Llagostera and villages nearby, Font-rubí and the Ribes valley—that is, in most of our domains. The *borda,* as at Esclet and Ganix, was a lesser manse or appendage. The vineyard (*vinea*), although it might form part of the domestic complex, is represented as a heritable holding in itself at Valmala, Llagostera and vicinity, and in the Ribes valley. The orchard (*ortus*) and *pariliata,* the latter referring to a measure of cultivated land plowed by paired beasts, figure at Gavà and Sant Climent; the *ferragenal* at Cabra was a planted enclosure for the forage of horses and other animals. Other bits of rural possession were the land (*terra*), perhaps vaguely equivalent to manse or

9. See Emmanuel Le Roy Ladurie, *Montaillou: village occitan de 1294 à 1324* (Paris, 1975); tr. Barbara Bray, *Montaillou: Cathars and Catholics in a French Village, 1294–1324* (London, 1978), chs. 2, 3.

inheritance, the field (*campus*), parcel (*fexa*), and "piece of land" (*pecia terre*). The term *alodium* (*alaudium*) could be applied generally to peasant property, as at Font-rubí and Gavà, where it possibly implied unrestricted possession or inheritance. Most forms of real property, chiefly the manse, *borda*, *domus*, and vineyard, figured in a structure of lordship with its own terminology. So the *honor* held from the Lord-Count is found at Gavà and Cabra. Hospitality (*alberga*) for the lord's men was the subject of regulation at Terrats, its abuse at Font-rubí and (though unspecified) perhaps also elsewhere was bitterly resented. And the bailiwick (*baiulia*), meaning custody or protection of tenure and also subject to abuse, is likewise widely attested.[10]

So far I have drawn on the memorials of complaint for evidence of broadly similar conditions in the dynastic lands of Barcelona. There is much by which to associate these people, a small population after all, in our perspectives of historical comprehension. But it hardly follows that the subjects of a common inquiry imposed from above meant to reveal themselves uniformly, nor were they required to do so. To judge from their patronymics, the peasants recorded were overwhelmingly of local birth and residence. The scribes were working with people in habitats, so to speak. And this means that as I move beyond numbers and names toward the more problematic aspects of status, kinship, and possession, I must reckon with the danger that a descriptive vocabulary of common terms may conceal regional peculiarities. Can one pry beyond these terms? Meet these people *in* their habitats?

10. See in general Joan Vilà Valentí, *El món rural a Catalunya*. Biblioteca de Cultura Catalana 6 (Barcelona, 1973), chs. 1–4; *FAC*, i, 28–49; and in the perspective of social formation, Josep M. Salrach, "La renta feudal en Cataluña en el siglo XII: estudio de las honores, censos, usos y dominios de la casa de Barcelona," *Estudios sobre renta, fiscalidad y finanzas* . . ., ed. Manuel Sánchez Martínez (Barcelona, 1993), pp. 29–70.

Old Domains: Caldes de Malavella, Llagostera, and Vicinity

Ermengallus and his brother-in-law, *Maria Guitarda* (was hers one of the rare matronymics?), *Petrus Uitalis:* these people and their households, their backs to woodlands and hills between them and a rocky coast a few kilometers to the southeast, looked out across fields of barley and wheat to the Pyrenees. Lots of them did. About 150 of them are named in the memorial of c. 1150 for Caldes and Llagostera, or by another count roughly 136 households; and the latter number might be multiplied by four or five to approximate a minimum local population of five hundred to seven hundred souls. In reality, these numbers must be too low in light of the scribe's testy declaration that his items for Caldes were not even "a tenth part" of the total, and his remark in another place that there had formerly been a hundred prosperous young men in the two villages. This was a comparatively large population, the largest agrarian settlement represented in any of the memorials of complaint.

It was also among the oldest. These peasants lived in domains that had been continuously inhabited and exploited since the ninth century. Once part of the fiscal patrimony of Girona, the tenancies at and around Caldes and Llagostera were a prize inheritance of the counts of Barcelona. They lay just east of the road from Barcelona to Girona and the northeast, the strategic artery of a dynastic entourage with interests in Provence. This location explains much of the economic vitality that rings through the memorial, not much about structures of habitation. It is manses and *bordae* we hear about, not houses. But the manses of this habitat surely were buildings as well as units of farming and taxation: plain stone and timbered farmhouses of two or three rooms and simple cabins. They would have been partly aggregated near the churches of Santa Maria and Sant Esteve in Caldes and of Sant Feliu in Llagostera, and partly scattered about the fields and vineyards. These dwellings, ever after crumbling and being rebuilt, would have seemed more opulent than the tiny houses adjoining Sant Esteve of Caulès in the hills just south of Llagostera. Caulès, already outmoded in a safer twelfth century, its children (perhaps including some named to us?) dispersed in the livelier plain below, vegetated and was abandoned in the fourteenth century.

Much as our perspective is distorted by my sources' insistence on the Lord-Count's protectorate, it is possible to see how the manse was fundamental to the peasants of Caldes and its vicinity. It was house and livestock and tools, and it was wealth. When *Nonar*'s son had 20s. taken by Arnal de Perella, "his manse remained deserted." This may seem puzzling, until we reflect that 20s. was about seven times the value of a pig, which was the basic rental imposed on manses by the Lord-Count. *Maienca* and her sons not only lost their manse to Arnal but also 30s., and then 8s. more "for protection" of the "manse where they now live." Only at Esclet, where Berenguer Mir was charged with depriving the Lord-Count of his services, do we hear of a tenure—in this case a half-*borda*—being sold; and it is clear that in these domains the obligations were thought more important than the house and land. Whether the peasants thought the manse (or *borda*) was familial property, like money or moveables, is not easy to say, but there is no mention of customary right in these domains.

One measured status by the manse. *Raimundus Guilelmi* was described as Arnal's manse-tenant (*mansuarius*) when he and his sons paid 9s. and were (even so?) ejected from the town. Later I shall have to question how far Arnal de Perella had managed to displace Count Raimund Berenguer IV in their shared lordship. What matters here is that possession under comital protection was probably less precarious than it seemed when in Arnal's hands. The *pagenses* in this habitat were as free as they were dependent. That was their privilege, in fact their only privilege in the 1150s, when the fiscal survey by Bertran de Castellet showed how they paid for it in prescribed renders: not only the "comital pig," but also a portion of the harvest (*tascha,* probably one-eleventh), a nut-bearing tree in each manse, and one laying hen per manse at Llagostera.

The equivocal freedom of peasants in these old domains of public authority would hardly call for notice were it not for an arresting curiosity of this habitat. All human freedoms are qualified. Not all are for sale. But in the memorial of complaints from Caldes de Malavella and Llagostera a considerable number of men and women troubled by Arnal de Perella are said to be "sold": *uendita* or *uenditus,* according to gender; that is, to have *been* sold. So, "from the sold daughter of *Bernardus Orucii",* Arnal has exacted 12s.; "from *Petrus Mascurd* sold 7[s.]," etc., for totals of ten men and ten women. On their face these allusions have the looks of a device of Arnal de Perella's petty financial tyranny. I shall return to them. What is of interest here is the possibility that altered or worsened status is in question.

Was it that something like the freedom of these peasants was being sold? One item seems virtually to say so: "Arnal de Per. sold the aforesaid *Petrus Arnallus de Aqua viva*'s wife for 10s. which she [he?] owed him." Could this be a case of bondage resulting from indebtedness, a case of slavery? If so, this was a general phenomenon in these domains—and uniquely so there and then. Or was it a scheme of Arnal's to brand some who ran afoul of him in village affairs brought to the justice he managed? Either way—and I have no better explanations to offer—it seems unlikely that these "sold" men and women established, let alone carried on, a status of social or legal bondage amidst the customary dependents of the Lord-Count. But it may not have been for want of trying on the part of those with power. And there was a good deal to tempt them in these domains.

They were a microcosm of economic diversity, prosperity, and growth. The peasants cultivated grains, but they also raised pigs and chickens. Some of them worked vineyards and made wines, both red and white. A few of them must have tended the forges and

mills in which the Count's bailiff collected fees or shares. And at
least four men were labelled "weaver" (*testor*), which points clearly
to some measure of specialization in labor while confirming my
sense of numbers and growth. *Poncius* the clerk, possibly attached to
the parish of Santa Maria, seems to have kept his own account of
seizures that mark him as a wealthy man. He lost 35s. "and another
time" 12[s.] and when the Count of Urgell was holding Caldes he
lost 91s. and 25 sextars of wheat and "another time 12s. and a
cover-cloth and 7 pigs." And when he squabbled with his brother,
Arnal de Perella had excuse to relieve him of another 30s.

Few if any other peasants lost this much, but the case of *Poncius*
the clerk is typical as a pointer to the kind of wealth accumulating
in these villages. *Ermengallus de Cantalupis* lost "three excellent coverlets and a donkey worth 20s." as well as 101s.; *Maria Guitarda*
lamented a 3s. pig. But most people were deprived of money in
amounts ranging from 2s. to 30s., and averaging about 9s. for all
reported seizures in Caldes and Llagostera. No doubt more of these
claims point to equivalencies in livestock or other goods than is
indicated, but it looks as if most peasants had coined money to lose.
Some even had morabetins, gold coins of Muslim derivation then
worth around 7s. of current silver pennies.

Can this liquidity be associated with buying and selling? While
there is no mention of a market as such, accounts of 1160 and after
refer to meat and grain as virtual commodities and to the Count's
share in toll and measuring-fee at Girona, ten kilometers to the
north. What seems certain is that peasant enterprise in the villages
was oriented to the demands of travel. Feed-grain (*cibaria*) was
available, iron-works for the equipping of knights and horses, and
an abundance of chickens and pigs. If people could be bought and
sold and weavers of cloth employed, I cannot doubt that some of
the money reported lost came to peasants from sales beyond household needs. But it was exchange out of the manse, so to speak. The
Count and his men drew on the renders of his peasant manses, but
they also exploited manses of their own directly; Arnal de Perella

was said to have consumed wine which his predecessor was used to exchanging for feed-grain. Moreover, the monks of Amer, Sant Daniel of Girona, and Casserres, even the lately established Templars, found it convenient to have their manses at Caldes by the Count's leave. These may have served as hostelries. The most lucrative trade was in lordship. Committing himself to Arnal de Perella and his devices, the poor peasant *Bernardus Viues* got rich.[11]

Old Domains II: the Ribes Valley

Quite a different habitat was the Ribes valley. Here *Guilelmus de Nogér* and the widow *Gitarda* and others like them lived in rustic homesteads scattered in uplands ranging from 900 to 1600 meters in altitude, overhung by pine-clad slopes and peaks. They breathed fresher—or sometimes, I imagine, smokier—air, fished and dammed faster, colder streams. Some of their manses must have been agglomerated around churches in Ribes, Pardines, and Queralbs (with several other vills), but dispersed residence was the norm. This, too, was an old settlement, originally dependent on the counts of Cerdanya, and since 1117 the domain of their successors of Barcelona. Here again the manse and *borda* were prevailing structures of habitation, no doubt chiefly because comital authority tended to impose itself in that way in the only records we have. The old practice of distinguishing between tributary and lordly (demesne) tenures is conspicuous in the Ribes area.

But the valley's population must have been smaller, perhaps much smaller, than that of the villages south of Girona. The boom time had long since passed. People had left the mountains as the Muslim threat subsided, lured by warmer fertile lowlands and en-

11. On Caldes de Malavella, Llagostera, Esclet, Ganix, and vicinity, see C-Ll-2501, E-G29; also Manuel Riu and Josefina Roma, *Excavaciones en el poblado medieval de Caulers, Mun. Caldes de Malavella, prov. Gerona*. Excavaciones arqueologicas en España 88 (Madrid, 1975); *FAC*, i, 174–177; ii, nos. 10,DE, 18; and *CR*, v (1991), 42–52, 185, 291–297.

larged opportunities. The memorials record complaints from some twenty-eight individuals and their relations at Ribes and Pardines and another twenty at Queralbs. This total of forty-eight persons may bear some correspondence to the forty-eight manses and twenty *bordae* specified in a contemporary survey of the Lord-King's domain in Ribes, but the latter were explicitly demesne tenures, leaving it uncertain how many other manses should be presumed to exist. Some other clues about this may help. In a remarkable record of 1158, at once survey and account, the *honor* of Ribes was charged with seventy-three "comital pigs" plus ninety-two ham-sides (*pernes*) amongst other obligations. And in the post (August)-1162 survey already mentioned some sixteen manses are identified with their tenants at the vills of Cuczág and Pardines, none of which correspond to tenancies recorded in the memorials of complaint.[12] So it looks as if the mentions of persons and tenures in the Ribes valley fall far short of approximating a total population. Perhaps the most indicative number is that of ninety-two *pernes*, for the ham-side was the basic imposition on manses in the nearby vill of Campelles.[13] Yet even if this number is appropriately multiplied to account for all who lived in these upland manses, I arrive at fewer than five hundred people.

What right in their manses these peasants believed they had is hard to see. As at Caldes and Llagostera the identity of building and manse is not very clear. The only mention of a *domus* relates to a house broken into. This suggests that a smoky shelter in the mountains might be worth less than its contents, while telling us nothing of the family within. A manse could be rendered worthless by the loss of (its?) oxen, as we have seen. Yet it was alleged that Raimund de Ribes "took" (or "stole"?—*abstulit*) manses, vineyards, and a field. This must mean that he placed them in his own lordship or direct domain (*dominicum*), as was said explicitly in two instances,

---

12. *FAC,* ii, nos. 15, 7.
13. ACA, Cancelleria, perg. extrainv. 3177.

appropriating their services at the Lord-King's expense. What is left unclear is whether some peasants "owned" their manses more fully than others who were rightfully in the old comital domains or dependent on religious houses or other lords. At any rate many free peasants, certainly those who lamented exactions on the occasions of children dying or daughters marrying elsewhere, were becoming subject to customary constraints on inheritance and marriage. These were customs of lordship born of economic concern to preserve the integrity of productive units.

People worked in the manses, and out of them, variously. Some tended the alluvial fields sown in grains unspecified (*blad*), surely both feed-grain and wheat. The high value placed on oxen would seem to confirm the importance of this labor, as does the existence of mills at Ribes, Queralbs, Pardines, and Ventalà. Vines on south-facing slopes were evidently valued enough to be seized, probably for producing wine for limited local consumption. Perhaps most labor, and much of it by women, went into raising sheep, pigs, and chickens, and making cheese. Spring lambs as well as hams and chickens figured among basic renders to the Lord-Prince. Fish and game turn up as tenurial obligations in neighboring domains, so probably also in Ribes.[14] As for domestic industry I find no clue in appellatives such as *testor* at Caldes de Malavella; but cloth was surely made also in the Ribes valley. There was a "cloth mill" (*molendinum draparium*) in one manse, which rendered "annually 30s. of revenue." This seems to be one of the earliest mentions of a water-driven fulling mill anywhere in western Europe.[15]

There is an unmistakable appearance of wealth in this upland habitat. Not so much in the incidence of property lamented, like blankets, clothing, tools, vessels, and livestock, as in money. Most

14. *FAC,* ii, no. 1LMNOP; i, 183–186.
15. See Josep M. Salrach, *El procés de feudalització (segles III-XII).* Història de Catalunya, vol. 2 (Barcelona, 1987), p. 431; *The Cambridge Economic History of Europe,* ii, ed. M. M. Postan and Edward Miller, 2d ed. (Cambridge, 1987), 669–670.

people reported pecuniary losses in amounts averaging much higher than in the lowlands: over 25s., roughly calculated, in the several vills. But here especially it would have been peasants with means, or savings in their little vulnerable chests, who reported losses. Even so, one or two claimed reduction to a poverty that must then have been as usual as it is now hard to discern. The heavy hand of Raimund de Ribes imposed a form of exchange in itself. Rustic production spilled over beyond the needs of subsistence. *Petrus Amad* said that Raimund de Ribes once took 10s. from him "because I had bought 3 quarters of grain from a man of Guardia." Here again supply to travelers may help to explain allusions to money in the complaints.[16]

Barcelona's Second Hinterland

Barcelona was doubly walled in the Middle Ages: first, by her built walls and second, by an outer perimeter of hills extending, with ample gateways to the west and east, from Montjuich to Montcada. In the twelfth century one could have looked down from Tibidabo as on a distant city, its houses and gardens spilling over the crumbling Roman fortifications into the tilted plain. This was a fertile and prospering hinterland oriented economically toward the city and its ecclesiastical lords. It was not a domain of the lord-counts, whose local revenues sprang from urban rents, tolls, and markets.[17] The early counts and their retinues had felt no need to dominate this near hinterland, a suburb they could easily traverse in a first day out from the city. Once over or through the wall of hills, a second hinterland opened out in old settled agrarian plains long subject to the counts of Barcelona. Here lay three of the domains whose

16. On Ribes and its environs, R1–3433, R2–3217; *FAC,* ii, nos. 1, 7, 15, 55, 131; i, 185–186; *CR,* x (1987), 45–50, 180–188, 192–201.

17. On which see Stephen P. Bensch, *Barcelona and Its Rulers, 1096–1291.* Cambridge Studies in Medieval Life and Thought, 4th series 26 (Cambridge, 1995), chs. 2–4.

peasants, when asked, protested abuses: Gavà, Sant Climent, and Viladecans, considered as a single domain in the Llobregat delta; Terrassa in the heart of what is today called the west Vallès; and Corró on higher ground in the east Vallès. Valmala can be considered an extension to this cluster if I am right in placing it in Osona, some forty kilometers north of Corró. Even closer beyond the Vallès to the northwest lay Castellvell de Rosanes, in hills about twenty-five kilometers from Barcelona.

Geographical rather than human space, this sprawling meandering hinterland defies comparison with the old rural habitats to the east and north. The memorials name peasants aggregated in three or four localities of similar natural conditions yet so distant from one another as to form distinct domains. Together with the delta the Vallès was an anciently and continuously settled zone that had suffered in the past from Muslim armed incursions and was disrupted yet again by the Almoravids in 1115. Conceivably there was a better continuity of habitation in the more remote domains like Corró and Valmala, but about this as about so much else the memorials are mute. How long had *Guilelmus Iohanis* and his family been settled at Corró? What had they in common with *Bernardus Oller* at Terrassa or with *Petrus Uedre* at Gavà? Could *Guilelmus Sancius* at Terrassa have had an Aragonese father? They all lived under skies we see night-lighted in the glow of greater Barcelona, yet in their days (and silent nights) they were hardly less remote in their rusticity than the valley-dwellers of Ribes.

Possibly they were distinct in one respect: a semblance of associative identity. It is "peasants" of the "village [*uilla*] of Gavà and Sant Climent" whose grievances are recounted; "people [*homines*] of Terrassa"; "enfranchised men [*franchearii*]" of Corró. And it may be that the men complaining were seen to personify their neighborhoods more than those at Caldes de Malavella, Llagostera, and the Ribes valley, for they were fewer in numbers. Some sixteen peasants were named at Gavà, Sant Climent, and Viladecans; twenty-eight at Terrassa; and only five at Corró, for a total of

forty-nine in these three domains. It is true that a further thirty-two
are listed at Valmala, but the memorial-quasi-survey for that obscure domain has an aura of completeness quite absent from those
for Gavà, Terrassa, and Corró. For these four domains might be
estimated a population equivalent to that of the Ribes valley, which
would surely be too low. It is a real possibility that fewer peasants in
these nearer comital domains had grievances than those south of
Girona and in the Pyrenees. Quite certainly the comital lands of
the Vallès were more densely settled than the memorials indicate.
No records of grievance survive for Caldes de Montbui and Vilamajor, major domains of Count Raimund Berenguer IV located
respectively east and west of the valley road from Barcelona to
Osona that passed near Corró. But it is possible to compare the
indicators of population for these places with those for Gavà-Sant
Climent-Viladecans, all of which were surveyed by Bertran de
Castellet in 1151. By count of manses and aggregated renders, the
survey-charters suggest totals of 128 tenures at Vilamajor and ap-
purtenances, 25 at Caldes, and 144 at Gavà and associated vills, or
197 households in all. This seems more like it. For these domains
plus Terrassa and Corró I can estimate a population of 2000–2300,
a number even larger than that of the Count's settlements south of
Girona, while doubtless much smaller than the aggregate population, dependent on other lords as well as on the Count or King, of
this "second hinterland" of Barcelona.

The memorials and fiscal surveys distort our view of agrarian
exploitation in these domains. In their lordly perspective the *honor*
at Gavà and Sant Climent looks like the manse, which is not
mentioned there but figures conspicuously at Terrassa and Corró.
Villa, honor, and manse in these places and at Castellvell look like
administrative expressions of older parcellary regimes, of micro-
properties which persist in the pariliate and orchard (*ortus*) at Gavà
and the vineyard, field, and terrace (*fexa*) at Valmala. In these lands
the impress of official lordship had probably weakened the claims

of proprietary right. *Bertrandus* of Sant Climent protested house-breaking together with seizures of maintenance in the "Count's vills"; but there is little else to point to insistence on the inviolable *domus* there or at Terrassa. Only at Lower Corró, where pillaged manses seem to have consisted of house, animals, and moveables, can I suppose that prosperous peasants like *Pages* and *Arnallus de Valoria* felt threatened in their inheritances.

These men of Corró may have been freer than their peers in neighboring domains. But the imprecision of their status rings through the charming ambiguity of their declaration that "we enfranchised people are his your men." Freedom went with dependence, the warrant of protection. Security of possession was what mattered here. A more precarious freedom, or its vestige, may be glimpsed at Terrassa, where *Petrus Arberti de Oliuariis* was identified as the son of a tenant given to Santa Cecilia of Montserrat by Count Raimund Berenguer III (1096–1131). This tenant had been given "together with his manse," implying an extent of lordly ownership unique in the memorials. But I think it likely that here as in other old comital domains the power to convey lordship of tenancies was acknowledged by peasants inclined to observe that their injuries were afflictions suffered by the Lord-Count or Lord-King. While tenurial conditions varied in these habitats, the peasants of the Llobregat-Vallès corridor, as also in Valmala, were customary tenants owing varied but moderate renders, often termed *census* (perhaps more like "token-payment" than "rent"), for holdings at once precarious and protected. I find no complaint here of a custom bearing on inheritance.

The economies of these domains sprang from varied household production. When *Bernardus Mironis* tried to keep Guilelm de Sant Martí's men out of his vineyards at Gavà, they took ten quarters of barley from him. Guilelm may have tried to organize a demesne-working of his own, imposing (or usurping?) carting services on peasants and seizing their donkeys; but the cultivation of barley, wheat, and feedgrains must have been carried on individually everywhere in the Vallès as well as at Gavà. Chickens and pigs were close about the houses. At Corró *Guilelmus Guitardi* was said to have lost seventeen sheep. *Gerallus de Fabrica* and his brother *Petrus* held the Count's forge for an annual render of one bull, which suggests the herding of cattle. Given the identity of name(s) and function in the latter case, I think it likely that *Bonetus ferrarius* and *Bernardus ferrer* at Terrassa were smiths or sons of smiths.

In these places again there was enough buying and selling to put money in peasant hands. Doubtless these people, like the valley-men of Ribes, had their coffers to hide, so it may simply point to variant styles of violence that seizures of money were reported chiefly at Terrassa. Here the average of some nineteen alleged occasions was around 28s. (or 18s., if I exclude an outlier claim of 200s.); that is, amounts comparable to those recorded in the Ribes valley. But even at Terrassa figure seizures of sheep, chickens, pigs, and grains, which were the notably vulnerable goods at Gavà and, almost exclusively so, in Valmala. The latter domain has all the appearance of tenurial subjection and poverty. Lacking reports from Caldes de Montbui and Vilamajor, it is hard to affirm quite the variety of productive pursuits visible in the villages near Girona. But the great hinterlands of Barcelona were not only comparably wealthy, but also more thickly settled and more numerous, the subject of no fewer than five survey charters in the inquiry of 1151. *R. Arnalli, Petrus Isarn,* "Peasant" himself (*Pages*) at Corró: people like these labored in the heartland of the old county of Barcelona, unwilling to trade the lessening danger of external invasion for the bullying of men who pretended to act for the Lord-Count.[18]

18. On the hinterland domains around Barcelona, G3451, Ter3275, V3202, Co3214. The corresponding survey charters of 1151 are in *FAC,* ii, no. 1ABCDQ. See also *CR,* xviii (1991), 54–64, 226–230, 325–326, 353–354; xx (1988), 56–83, 300–305, 405, 419. A major study of this habitat can be found in Mercè Aventín i Puig, *La societat rural a Catalunya en temps feudals. Vallès oriental, segles XIII–XVI* (Barcelona, 1996).

The Old Frontier: Font-rubí

The enterprise of this heartland had long since spread westward, across the Llobregat into the Anoia valley and the Penedès. These places were ceasing to be a land of hucksters and "perverse men," as the monks had spoken of it when the Moors seemed close and terrifying. The counts of Barcelona had men and allies settled there for more than a century when the troubles alleged by peasants at Font-rubí unfolded. Some of these men were in charge of castles in an accidented terrain of *puigs* (Latin: *podium*), and one of these castles was Font-rubí, located on a *puig* backed in the Serra of Ancosa and opening southeastward to the plain. The master of this castle and others like him were among the busiest visible people in this habitat in the years from 1150 to 1165. In fact, I count more of them than working peasants in the pertinent memorials of complaint. For this anomaly it is tempting to scold the scribes, who for once named so few victims. But they had their reasons.

Font-rubí was a different place. It was hardly yet a domain, this outcropping of an old frontier. Bertran de Castellet had not thought it worth surveying in 1151, when Piera to the east was still only a 34-pig domain, and Vilafranca in the plain even smaller. Clustered down the slopes from the castle, Font-rubí was not so much an ordered lordship of manses as a few hardy homesteaders claiming the Lord-Count's protection against the strong armed men up the hill and ever clattering by. They claimed to be "your man" (that is, the Count's), like *Raimundus Marti* and his kinsman *Berengarius,* who cultivated barley with oxen; or *A. Compan,* who dealt in wheat. *Iohanes bonus homo* and *Carbo de Fonte rubeo* had money to lose. *P. Compan* deplored the inopportune seizure of a mare used in threshing, while *Martinus de Fonterubeo,* blessed and cursed with possession of ample lodgings, suffered them to be commandeered by force. *Bernad Gilabert* had pack animals and horses. And if I add *Giu* (?) the clerk, said to have been beaten in the mostly illegible later complaints, it is to set before us the sum total of peasants or victims identified in the several memorials for Font-rubí.

Not much of a haul, these nine named people. Nor does it really help to add the sixteen or so names of those accused, other than to suggest that such a lavish array of knightly tormentors cannot have suffered from any shortage of peasants to abuse. There were many more people at Font-rubí than we know of from the memorials given over chiefly to specifying transgressions and their perpetrators. Overcrowded houses are evoked more than once. Even so, this must have been a smaller population than in some other habitats I have described, perhaps fewer than 250 souls. Their holdings as elsewhere could be described as manses or alods; more than elsewhere the house (*domus, kasa*) was valued, its violation deplored.

Here for once may be discerned the relation of shelter to the extended family. There seems to have been a complaint about efforts to peg the *census* to inhabitants rather than units of habitation, a practice evidently to be resisted by "ten brothers in one house [*mansio*]" who understood the custom to be one pig per tenure. And since the habitation in this case was explicitly termed "alod" (*alaudium*), it seems safe to say that house (*domus, mansio*), manse (*mansus*), and alod were overlapping expressions in their semantic field. In a climate lurching from torrential rains to harsh aridity, the mud and stone shelters for people and beasts were prized properties, doubtless well filled, and all too vulnerable to the needs of armed and mounted men. Hospitality was their demand, not their right; I see no sign of regulated maintenance, such as at Terrats.

This may have been at the root of disorders around Font-rubí. Perhaps even more acutely than tenants in the older easterly domains, these people worried about their status, defended their customary liberties. They were free indeed who could claim that "in the days of our fathers we had the sort of manses that were paying" only one sheaf and one basketful of feedgrain apiece. And their apprehension had even more to do with personal status than with economic franchise. They equated forced hospitality with servility, exclaiming in their memorial of the 1160s that Berenguer de Bleda and his castellans were compelling them to render hospitality "like slaves" and, worse, demanding them to confirm his right to judge his charge that they had resisted. Forced into carrying service for journeys to Barcelona, Anglesola, and Tortosa, all distant places, they were offered to "friends" of their masters "like captives," a simile that vividly confirms the atmosphere of collective alarm over perceived threats of disparagement. Nor was this all. The injuries alleged at Font-rubí were deplored as acts of "dishonor," of personal as well as social disparagement. Not only did the tormentors "dishonor us and our wives," not only did they "beat us wickedly," they repeatedly "cut" or "pulled our beards." The meaning of this sort of violence will be examined in later chapters, but one facet of it matters here. The people in this habitat clung to the perilous freedom their parents had won by moving to this rugged frontier. They or their scribes were readier than their peers in older domains to define their status collectively, and so perhaps to "write off" individual losses of property and money for social recognition.

Too few persons are named to provide a clear sense of occupational identity and wealth. Two people bore the castle's name (*de Fonte rubeo,* literally: "bramble-spring"), which may suggest that other people lived below the walls (or, in other words, that *incastellamento,* the flight to the safety of hilltop fortification, was here incomplete). This is what I would expect of a diverse micro-economy. Some peasants may have trudged down from their houses to work fields in barley and wheat; vines grew on nearly slopes as well as below. But the manses as elsewhere concentrated labor, nurturing chickens, pigs, and sheep; producing cheeses; tending orchards and gardens. The ham-side hung in these houses, too. No wonder strong men were tempted to move in on people, to help themselves to sacks and break into casks. And if peasants were requisitioned for transport, it was surely because they were equipped with horses and donkeys and the appropriate services to local travel. The sharpening-fee (*lozet*), some lamented, had been doubled from two quarters of barley to four or even five "by the measure of La Granada." People evidently traded at La Granada, a possession of the bishop of Barcelona, and at La Guardiola in the plain below.

Their wealth was chiefly in barley, wheat, and money (*diners*). The early memorial addressed to Count Raimund laments above all else the newly-imposed tallage (*questas*) in these items; and there are other indications that sacks of grain were virtually as current— and as vulnerable—as coined money. The *lozet* was imposed in barley, as we have seen. Perhaps there was less coined money in circulation than in the older domains, for average reported losses in specie were under 20s. for only five or six occasions. Something of the value of Font-rubí derived from its potential for development together with Vilafranca in the great plain to the south, which grew in population and wealth enormously in the later twelfth century. And there was a living to be made in supply to an expanding traffic westward.[19]

A Further Frontier: Cabra, Argençola

Yet another frontier was opening to development beyond the mountains of Montmell and Ancosa. The two villages voiced in my final three memorials were located in high places of its eastern borderlands: Cabra (elevation: 493 meters) dominating the pass from the plain of Tarragona into the Conca de Barberà, and Argençola (650 meters) some thirty kilometers north at the confluence of the rivulets Clariana and Molí. These places can have had little in common save fading traditions of Muslim devastations—plus one more urgent thing: grievances against a baron named Berenguer de Clariana, who for his part knew both places well.

19. On Font-rubí, F1-3409, F2-3141, F3-3288; *FAC,* i, 207–208; *CR,* xix (1992), 28–70, 116. On the matter of castles, see below, p. 64.

In both places the powerful seem to muscle out the people. The afflicted are named, it is true, more of them than at Font-rubí: *Raimundus Dondara* and *n'Aiculina d'Almenara* among some eighteen people at Cabra, and at Argençola *Berengarius Bonfill* and *Amallus Oromir* along with eleven others. But in these habitats the history of settlement is obscured by the disruptions of a turbulent frontier. Castles seem to cast longer shadows; the memorials tell of their masters and knights as well as of peasants: of Guilelm de za Ciresa and Guilelm de Concabella at Cabra and of the inscrutable Berenguer de Aguiló at Argençola. Not unlike cowboys of the range, such men helped mold new habitats deeply marked by the fortunes of power.

Cabra had been a fortified outpost of the early county of Barcelona. In the eleventh century it came into possession of the monks of San Martino de Albenga, who were less than ideally situated (in Italy!) to keep it up. It seems to have been long derelict, described in the twelfth century as a "habitation for wild animals," when Christian knights moved in at the expense of *mudejar* peasants and monastic rights alike. In 1160 Count Raimund Berenguer IV posed as the restorer in an agreement with Albenga, securing two-thirds of the lordship over Cabra and sanctioning a domain in this defensible upland adjoining fertile plains then in full tide of resettlement. Of Argençola even less is known. Its castle left traces in the records of Sant Cugat, whose monks had the lordship; but it too had been ruined by the Muslims and nothing is heard of it for more than a century after 1032. Only with the memorial of complaints dating from the 1180s does life here become visible, bursting into view as the "people of Argençola" appealed to the King at the instance of their own castellan against the depredations of the violent lord of Clariana nearby.[20]

The relation of habitation to fortifications is problematic at Cabra, unknown at Argençola. Most likely peasant dwellings at

20. Ca1–2609, Ca2–3474, A3145.

Cabra were dispersed below a castle that may have been too con-
stricted or dilapidated to admit of hilltop settlement. The castle
may have remained in disrepair as late as about 1173, when Bertran
de Vilafranca told of the king's "palace" being violated. Mean-
while, the monks of Sant Pere de Riudebitlles (near Font-rubí)
were exercising Albenga's share of the lordship and disputes arose
over the divided jurisdiction of a growing but dispersed settlement.
In 1194 the King and the Prior chartered the "settlers" (*populatores*)
by permitting *and requiring* them to "live together in the village on
Cabra hill" on condition of paying an annual fixed tax of one
hundred morabetins to be shared by the lords.[21] It is clear that
habitation in dispersed vills below the summit had been a cause of
controversy, not at all clear what became of the old castle in the
larger (fortified?) complex loosely termed *villa* and *castrum*. As for
Argençola, I can only imagine that the "people" who complained
were scattered well outside their castle's walls, victimized in their
vulnerable possessions, perhaps as their own castle burned.

   We see these people vividly yet very incompletely in memorials
unlike those for other domains and unlike each other. The misfortunes of some eighteen persons are recounted by the old bailiff of
Cabra; five of these are also named by his enemies in a second
memorial, plus another four. Most of these have the appearance of
substance, with honors to lose and grain, wine, and coined money.
And it may indeed have been the more prosperous who suffered in
a climate of knightly rivalry for influence. Anyway, it is harder than
ever to extrapolate numbers from those identified at Cabra. But the
lesson of the memorials together with the jurisdictional conven-
tions of 1187 and 1194 is surely that lordship in these domains was
valuable. The commuted tallage ordained in 1194 (one hundred
morabetins), if calculated in terms of the modest renders per manse
normal in older domains, would suggest a population of over two
hundred households, or perhaps a thousand people by that date.

21. *CPC*, i¹, no. 200; see also *FAC*, ii, no. 156.

No doubt it had grown, and was attracting settlers notably in the years to which the memorials refer. Argençola's population would have been smaller, possibly no more than the fifteen-odd households mentioned, plus an undisclosed number of Berenguer's knights.

As elsewhere, the peasants in these domains held lands, houses, and moveable posessions freely. The eccentric memorial of Argençola, which tells us more about household furnishings than any other, says nothing about the buildings which held them, except that some houses and walls were burned, or about the tenurial status of their possessors. I think it likely that they were tenants of Berenguer de Aguiló, a castellan lord, in alliance with the Lord-King against Berenguer de Clariana. Much more can be said about Cabra, where all is expressed in perspectives of lordly jurisdiction. Here bailiffs may have attempted to impose quasi-servile levies, as in the Ribes valley, such as the amend of adultery known as *cucucies* that is mentioned in passing. But the peasants' holdings we hear of, evidently not the least in value, were normally termed *honor* (and, in these records, never *mansus*). Peasants worked their own fields and vineyards, and some of them at least, such as "your man *Poncius de Barbera*," worked in the Lord-King's demesne farm (*dominicatura*). Prevailing efforts to increase obligations attaching to tenures may explain why some holdings are described as allodial (*alodium, alodio franc et chitio*). *Raimundus de Spina versa* was said to have lost a corral (*ferragenal*) "which he always held and possessed." Once only do we hear of a house (*domus*) broken into at Cabra, but all these people lived in houses of stone, wood, and wattle.

The people of Cabra cultivated the usual grains while producing, or trading in, wines on a larger scale than elsewhere. The memorials convey the impression of an economy integrated with trade and travel; grain, wine, and money being the principal commodities. The "men of Hostafrancs" complained of losing twenty mitgers of grain, while those of Tarragona and Montblanc figured as litigants or as the bailiff's allies. To judge from accusations against Bertran the bailiff, sales of good will as well as those of land were lucrative enough to promote pecuniary exchange as well as resentment. Of local industry or milling there is little hint. Wealth lay in "possessions" (*avere*) as well as in the honor, and it may be that losses of money and moveables could drive people from houses less venerable or prized than in the Old Catalonian domains. Bertran the bailiff had much to say about seizures of money, and the amounts in question were, on average, much higher than I have (roughly) calculated elsewhere: close to 80s. per occasion.

The economy of Argençola, on the other hand, defies description. All I can see is what its twelve peasant deponents claimed to have lost. The result is an itemized inventory as incomparably informative about household provisions and possessions as it is useless for the circumstances and dynamics of work and exchange. What is clear is that these people cultivated grains of all sorts, that they possessed wine in sufficient amounts to make it seem that they had lots of vines to tend, and that they raised chickens, pigs, and sheep. Theirs would seem to have been a system of work centered in the manse, which is mentioned in the account of *Berengarius de Vilanova* as something distinct from the *villa*. He is said to have lost "five houses," which I take to refer to buildings in his manse as well as in the vill.

The memorial's well arranged inventory begins with grains, of which the values are strikingly high. Thus eight men were said to have lost an average of more than twenty-seven mitgers of barley, or at prevailing prices roughly 54 to 75s. These were household stores of provisions, including substantial measures of feedgrain, wheat (*fru[mentum]*), wine, bacons, and chickens. *Berengarius Bonfill* claimed to have lost a horse, a plowshare, and an axe. Everyone itemized seizures of clothing, coverlets, towels, and other forms of cloth, shoes, pottery, and utensils for cooking and eating. The list could go on. It is safe to suspect that much of what peasants lamented in seizures elsewhere would have corresponded closely to what is exceptionally detailed here. The men of Argençola, as rustic and remote as any peasant society in twelfth-century Catalonia, lived in well stocked though doubtless sparsely furnished households. Enterprising people could make a living on this frontier as elsewhere. What they lacked was adequate protection from a society of castles with a different agenda.[22]

★ ★ ★

People in their habitats: it is not easy to say which made which. Did their common subservience to the Lord-Count of Barcelona counteract the particularities of place? Did their interrogators impose similar responses by asking identical questions? What differentiating influence did the behavior of those who troubled the peasants have? On the first of these questions the memorials have little to say other than the eccentric ones for Terrats and Valmala; but what little they do say accords with survey-charters of 1151 to suggest that obligations on manses and households were generally light and various. Comital lordship rested on traditions, customs, and negotiations of considerable diversity. As for the interrogations, I find so little uniformity in response as to make me think that scribes worked with hardly more than an oral mandate to secure the particulars of grievance and bring them to the Lord-Count's or Lord-King's court. So the most salient of these potential influences on habitat would seem to be the ways in which the peasants reported the actions of their tormentors. The differences in this perception will be considered in their place. What matters here is that the grievances attributed to named persons become inevitably an element of their historical identity.

Arnallus Ruscheti of Gavà lost 8s., according to Ponç the Scribe, and so did *Carbonellus* at Caldes de Malavella. This was about the average pecuniary loss reported at Caldes, but much less than that in the Llobregat delta. Seizures of grain in moderate amounts were

22. On Cabra, *LFM*, i, no. 254: "quod erat ferarum habitacio"; *FAC*, i, 214; on Argençola, *CSC*, ii, no. 442; iii, no. 1099; *CR*, xix, 365–366; *CC*, v, 161–164. On prices, *FAC*, i, 302–308.

reported in most of the habitats—from *P. Guilelmi* and *Bernardus Gilaberti* at Gavà and from *A. Compan* at Font-rubí, for example— yet it is impossible to affirm that such losses mark off these people as plowmen distinct from the many everywhere whose losses were reported in monetary terms. Other reports purport to say more of variable circumstances, without revealing identity very personally. At Caldes de Malavella *Poncius* the Clerk seems to have run afoul of Arnal de Perella by suing his (Ponç's) brother and then brawling with him; it cost him 30s. *Carbo de Fonte rubeo* "complains" against Berenguer de Bleda "that he took 33s. away from him . . . And at once Berenguera de Puigdàlber came [with her knights?] and broke into Carbo's house and increased the pledges [she already held?] to more than 15s. The aforesaid Berenguera did this because she was unable to have her right in those 33s." In these cases it looks as if men caught up in hazardous processes of justice were articulate enough—one was a priest—to engage the scribes in their stories of distress. At Argençola *Petrus de Caruiens* and eleven of his fellows, responsive to *their* scribe's peremptory questionnaire, seem virtually to open their storehouses, wine cellars, clothes hampers, and tool-sheds to our inspection. And when *Ermessen* told how Raimund de Ribes took 5s. from her and her husband *Esbaldíd* because (she said) "our little son died, no other reason," the record brings us close to sentimental identity. There are other such testimonies from the Ribes valley.

So these people seem to speak from variable circumstances. Their names, amplified and differentiated by their attributed griev-ances, remain to reflect upon. I have kept their names in original written forms not (of course) because these people spoke to one another in Latin but to avoid diluting the attenuated memory left to us from their experience across the centuries. The scribes, how-ever inadvertently, represented something of their subjects' dignity, of their social standing, by identifying so many of them and by enhancing their names, as a rule, in Latin dress. (How many *Guiems* or *Peres* might have been surprised to be shown *Guilelmus* or *Petrus* on the parchments?) Or even, at least once, the reverse: for in telling how *n'Aiculina d'Almenara* lost a pony, the bailiff Bertran conveys a whiff of polite spoken (Catalan) salutation, his form abbreviating *na* (*domna;* Latin: *domina*), meaning lady. It is fair to guess that the scribes were working in polite societies; that their subjects counted as somebodies, which is why they objected to having their beards pulled or cut; and that in an economic sense, as the evidence has already prompted me to suggest, these were peasants with property to lose. There is imposing presence in the reticent history of men owing *alberga* at Terrats: *Arnaldus Garriga . . . Martinus* likewise. *Berengerius* likewise,—and the rest. These men, like the "people" of Terrassa or the "good men" of Cabra, were "famous among the barns," and for all we know not less in their local standing than the "enfranchised men" of Corró.

And if people like these, the "peasants" (*pagenses*), "manse-holders," and "rustics" whose complaints fill the memorials, were (or had been) comparatively well off, it follows that house-trashings and persecutions such as *Guilelmus Iohanis* and *Alegretus Ferrarius* reported at Corró and Cabra respectively cannot have been suffered by all working people in these societies. Those at Font-rubí resented being treated "like slaves"; does this mean that slavery was known there or in those old domains where the cognomen *ma(n)cip* suggests that emancipation had been known to occur? Possibly some question about this remains in regard to Caldes de Malavella and Llagostera, but there is little else in the memorials to point to an underclass of bondmen in any of the Lord-Prince's domains. What I suppose is that a considerable population of unpropertied siblings and servants existed on the peripheries of the several microsocieties here in evidence. Some such people would have attached themselves to the households of barons and knights. In short, there were people unnoticed who, being unworthy of the best efforts of serious plunderers, did not figure among the people moved or induced to complain. These two elements represented the bulk of the rural populations in these domains. To these elements must be added that of magnates, lords and horsemen, who are not quite always among the alleged tormentors, who are mentioned in considerable albeit unspecific numbers, and who must in any case be reckoned an integral presence everywhere. If it seems hard to think of the Prior of Riudebitlles as an offender around Cabra, we should not forget that to maintain his claims to lordship in a zone of competing claims he relied upon faithful men in his service.

These considerations point to a somewhat larger aggregate population than the sum of totals for the several habitats I have suggested above. My rough estimates, set out in the accompanying table, are for a total of affected or afflicted peasants amounting to about 4075 in a larger rural population of fewer than twelve thousand. I need hardly insist on the fragility of such figures. The memorials as we have them are only incidentally records of habitation making no claim to completeness and sometimes expressly incomplete. Some of them intersect with fiscal records which prove that, while the memorials of complaint pertain to an original domain of public lordship extending from the eastern Pyrenees along the agricultural belt extending across the Llobregat into frontier lands, they do not fully correspond to those comital lordships. Thus, I estimate the Llobregat-Vallès cluster (memorials 2, 3, 9, and 10) as comparatively populous amongst domains recording complaints, yet very incomplete as an expression of comital lordship in that region. There is some reason to believe that the Lord-Count's men were taking account of his domains administratively in the last years of Raimund Berenguer IV, but their concern was with manses and, at best, injustice, not with population.[23] So I conclude that an affected population of several thousand peasants

23. *FAC*, i, ch. 2.

Estimated Populations in Comital Rural Domains, 1150–1165

Major Comital Domains	Estimates from Memorials	Estimates from Surveys, Accounts
Caldes de Montbui		400 (1B; i, 168)
Vilamajor		500 (1A; i, 172)
Tagamanent		250 (1A; i, 171)
Corró d'Avall	100 (Co3214)	100 (14; i, 169)
Terrassa	500 (Ter3275)	600 (1Q; i, 171)
Gavà	350 (G3451)	350 (1C; i, 169)
Sant Feliu (Llobregat)	300 (G3451)	300 (1D; i, 170)
Caldes de Malavella	500 (C-Ll-2501)	900 (1G; i, 174)
Llagostera	700 (C-Ll-2501)	1200 (1GH; i, 176)
Esclet, Ganix	75 (E-G29)	(75 E-G29)
Palau-sacosta		125 (1I; i, 178)
Palafrugell		250 (1J; i, 177)
Besalú		1200 (1K; i, 179)
Prats de Molló		500 (1L; i, 184)
Vilafranca de Conflent		1000 (1M; i, 193)
Terrats, Thuir	100 (Tts3283)	(100 Tts 3283; i, 189)
Cerdanya (Llívia)		500 (1N; i, 195)
Querol		150 (1,O; i, 197, 199)
Molló		600 (1P; i, 184)
Ribes	500 (R1–2 [3433, 3217])	600 (i, 186)
Valmala (terra)	200 (V3202)	(200 V3202)
Piera		250 (1E; i, 208)
Vilafranca del Penedès		100 (1F; i, 209)
Font-rubí	250 (F1–3 [3409, 3141, 3288])	(250 i, 207)
Argençola (?)	100 (A3145)	(100 A3145)
Cabra	400 (Ca1–2 [2609, 3474])	800 (i, 214)
Estopanyà		100 (5, 6, 9; i, 226)
TOTALS	4075	11,500 (11025)

This table attempts to relate an estimated population for the fourteen domains selected for their memorials of complaint with an estimated total population for some twenty-three major domains drawn substantially from other fiscal sources. The reader should understand that: (1) that some domains are represented only by memorials (middle column), others only by fiscal surveys or accounts (right-hand column, cited from *FAC*), still others by both types of record; (2) that in some of the latter cases (two or more records) one suggests a larger population than the other (e.g., Terrassa); and (3) that in cases where a memorial is our only comparable record, it is counted (in parentheses, right-hand column) as if it were a survey or account. *The figures are all speculative,* by necessity. They can do no more than suggest comparative orders of magnitude. The total population of comital tenants for all domains, including cities for which no comparable records survive, was much higher than shown here. Citations are to the memorials and to pertinent matter in *FAC*.

represented a considerable proportion—perhaps thirty-five percent?—of the Lord-Prince's rural tenants in Catalonia. It is a small
sample, to repeat, yet it gives voice to a substantial mass of a
twelfth-century population.

And it is in light of the likely distribution of persons working,
serving, fighting, and praying in the habitats that the difficulty of
knowing our subjects from recitations of their suffering can be
addressed. The problem is whether the narrations of violence and
seizure tell of normal life in these rural habitats or rather of something exceptional as well as deplorable. Do we know more about
Poncius or *Ermessen* or *Carbo* than about *Amallus Ruscheti* because
more is said of what happened to them? Or to put it differently,
were *Amallus* and his fellows in the Llobregat domains unlucky to
lose a few sous or sacks of grain?—or the reverse? These are harder
questions than may at first sight appear, even if I allow for evidence
already presented that other people suffered worse afflictions.
Much of this problem must be reserved for discussion of the norms
of power. But it is a problem of people as well as of power. For it
looks like a question whether our peasants lived in violent societies
as well as polite ones.

Looks like, I say, for it may now be timely to question whether
the afflicted subjects of this book lived in "societies" at all. I do not
mean to impose a recondite sociological test on this discussion. I
only mean to suggest that the alleged tormentors of peasants on the
Lord-Prince's lands seem not to have been very familiar to their
victims, let alone integrated with them socially. There is no reason
to suppose that the troubled peasants were prone to exercising the
violence they claimed to have suffered. They may have robbed or
cheated, as some people do; but they had recourse to customary
constraints and justice (to the profit of the Lord-Prince's vicars and
bailiffs), and there is nothing in the memorials to suggest that the
tormentors had learned their ways from the peasants. Most of the
people in these villages and valleys, including priests and monks,

were used to freedom and protection such as they associated with their traditions of pioneering dependence on Christian counts exercising Frankish royal power. Their habitats were open and extended, oriented to productive fields and slopes, uneasy with castles and their demanding denizens. Production meant the manse, the homestead; it meant service to those who exercised the Count's or the King's public lordship, but hardly dependence on them.

Yet it might be wrong to conclude that those denounced and feared were a class apart. The scribes said little, save of their deeds, to distinguish them at all. Guilelm de Sant Martí is an unqualified name in the account of violence he and Adalbert perpetrated at Gavà and Sant Climent. So are Deusde at Terrassa, Berenguer Mir at Esclet and Ganix, Dorca at Valmala, and Pere de Bell-lloc at Corró. Only by reading between the lines can I infer that Deusde, Arnal de Perella, and Raimund de Ribes held vicarial powers in their domains; only at Font-rubí are Berenguer de Bleda and others called "vicars." But the truth is that the scribes are exceedingly stingy with social or functional designations of any sort for those in power or alleged to have troubled people. "Nobles" are mentioned only in the memorial for Caldes and Llagostera, where "noble knights" elsewhere are credited with alluring persecuted peasants to their *honors*. "Knight" in this usage (*nobiles milites*) was a term of elite status, to be contrasted with that of "horsemen" (*kauallarii*) such as were denounced at Cabra. But lesser horsemen could also be called "knights" (*milites*) and could suffer loss themselves, as did those of Berenguer de Aguiló, whose lordship at Argençola (as described) would seem to exemplify the "honor of a noble knight." The critical social determinant, although the scribes never say so, must have been the possession of a horse and arms. That may have been all that distinguished one of Berenguer de Bleda's "men" or "horsemen" from the peasants whose houses they raided. The distinction must have been simply functional, one such as could separate brother from brother, for if any ceremony attached to the apprenticeship in arms in twelfth-century Catalonia, nothing survives to prove it.

The silence on this point, which extends to countless other records, may have meaning. Or it may not. But I do not think it safe to believe that the memorials unconsciously ignore (or misrepresent) social realities. Take the matter of castles. They are practically never mentioned. Nothing is said about the strongholds of Guilelm de Sant Martí, Deusde, Berenguer Mir, Raimund de Ribes, or Berenguer de Clariana. Arnal de Perella luxuriated in his "house" (*domus*), Berenguer de Bleda in his several houses. The Lord-King's "palace" at Cabra was violated. The castle which figures at Font-rubí was the hill-top settlement rather than the tower. Yet the scribes surely knew that the "castellans" of Berenguer de Bleda occupied fortified dwellings and towers; that Pere de Bell-lloc's prison was in his keep; that Berenguer de Clariana (and his adversary Berenguer de Aguiló) were the lords of castles. Then why the silence of the memorials? The answer, I believe, is that the scribes shared a perspective, broadly that of the peasants, in which the Lord-Prince's protective authority remained normative. They wrote allegations against people, not things, described violence without explaining it. Fortifications had some place in the habitats I have ventured to evoke, but castles or towers were not—not yet?—conceptualized socially as violent space. Roman fortifications were in ruins at Terrassa and Caldes de Malavella. So it is hard to say whether the castellans and knights were thought to be categorically different from those who suffered, whether by the victims or by themselves. It is they alone, if any, who were disposed to violence; it was assuredly they who so intimidated the people at Cabra that they "dared not" appeal against them. Were knights threatening?—or only some knights?

There were enough of them, even if not all knights were terrifying, to ensure that their habits bore heavily on the social outlook. Moreover, their needs like their habits of constraint may have been tempting or contagious; one became a horseman in these habitats by acting like one, perhaps not always mounted. Arnal de Perella seems a case in point; what is certain is that he, Raimund de Ribes, Guilelm de Sant Martí and their likes, could never have imposed or violated as they were charged without the collaboration of unnamed persons of ambiguous yet precarious status. Such circumstances impose their own dynamic, create expectations. People who lost 2s., like *Arnallus Rog* and *Dominicus Roi* at Caldes de Malavella, surely knew that others there claimed the seizures of much larger sums of money or valuables. Yet who can finally say whether they were comparatively lucky, when their scribe fails to indicate, unlike him who wrote in the Ribes valley, how poor they were?

Violence was familiar and constant in these medieval settlements, which is not quite to say that these were violent societies. The peasants who complained were responsive to questionnaires of peace and security; rich and poor, these were the peoples of their places, for whom work was no disgrace and violence was disorder. Theirs was the normative ethic. Their tormentors were not a class, nor yet a society in themselves, but mostly grasping aspirants to service and status. They were becoming the Other in societies of laboring tenants who were not lords.[24]

★   ★   ★

After all, it is not easy to know these people. They were once so much more than names and claims, once in no need of the conjectures I have heaped on their reluctant expressions of complaint. It would only foster an illusion to pretend that they typify some larger agrarian universe. On the contrary, I feel compelled to mark off their domains, holding the spotlight on *Arbertus de Pi* at Llagostera,

24. On the problem of violence, see also Chapter V.

Ramon Sunier at Pardines, and their fellows in old comital lands to the blacked-out exclusion of their neighbors in the lordships of the bishop of Girona or of the monks of Ripoll or Sant Cugat or of castellans of the roads from Barcelona to Girona, Vic, and Montserrat. Such tenants are known to have borne similar names and obligations, but much else of their circumstances eludes easy comparison for want of study. Might other lords have heard such complaints as Raimund Berenguer IV and his son?

Yet I cannot finally dissociate the peasants of our memorials from those unvoiced ones nearby. The natural surroundings they lived in have not changed much. Even allowing for the urban sprawl that has transformed Terrassa and the Llobregat delta, the craggy granitic escarpments remain; the vistas to more distant mountains or down valleys toward fertile plains. The toponymy of hill and vale was already affecting the proper names of my subjects—witness *A. de Plano, Petrus Bernardi de Podio albari,* and *Geral de Ual de Uila*—a tendency on its way to filling Barcelona's telephone book with *Pla, Puig, Serra, Vall,* and the like. But more than this, we know what these peasants looked like—or, more exactly, how an artist quite possibly associated with Girona cathedral imagined them.

The so-called "Tapestry of Creation" preserved at Girona and dating perhaps from a generation before the memorials can only confirm our image of an agrarian life of turned soils, trees, animals, and fish. One worked under a portentous Year and through the Seasons and Months, with Cold (*frigus*) allegorically blowing on the works of February, competing with the Sun's rays in March, before giving way to solar warmth in May and June. Much of the manse's technology figures in the horse-drawn four-wheeled cart of Sunday, the two-wheeled (two-horsed) plow of April, and sundry tools (scythe, fishing-rod, shovel). Through it all strides the peasant, energetic in his works, beardless (I note well), wearing caps and short cloaks and sometimes stockings. His facial expressions seem by turns resolute and pensive. He warms his feet and hands by Winter's fire.[25]

The wages of sin are toil in this "radiant vision of a lost Paradise," and the laborer, serenely marginalized in Creation's monumental story, lives on. "Cold pastoral." He is nameless here, unlike *Maienca* at Caldes, or *Petrus Ferren* who used to live at Cabanyes (also near Girona) and had a fine vineyard before he went to Tarragona. But there was something of Adam, who *is* named in Creation's Eden, in him—and in them.

25. Pere de Palol, *El Tapís de la Creació de la catedral de Girona* (Barcelona, 1986). The words quoted in the next sentence are from Bonnassie, *La Catalogne,* ii, 879.

Flight into Egypt. Santa Maria of Estany; capital sculpture, late twelfth century.

Memorial of Gavà, Sant Climent, and Viladecans, c. 1145–1150.
Original, ACA, Cancelleria, pergamins extrainventaris 3451.

Memorial of Corró, c. 1162–1170. Original, ACA, Canc., perg. extrainv. 3214.

Argençola, from the northeast.

"Tapestry of Creation," late eleventh century. Cathedral Treasury, Girona.

"Summer" (*Estas*), detail from "Tapestry of Creation."

Rachel and her flock. Santa Maria of Girona, capital sculpture, twelfth century.

Queralbs, Sant Jaume.

[III]

POWER

"*Poncius de Riu de péres* took away from a man *Puges* of Pardines a donkey worth 40s. for a debt of Raimund de Ribes. . . ." These words, laconic to the verge of ambiguity, come from the Ribes valley, but what do they mean? If I guess that *Puges* owed Raimund money, which seems safe, I still wonder how much. Is the donkey's valuation at 40s. meant to assert that the seizure was excused as a recovery, with or without interest? Or as a penalty for non-payment? For that matter, who is this *Poncius* who seizes a donkey "for a debt of Raimund de Ribes?" Was *Poncius* to blame when in the next clause it says that Raimund de Ribes took 10s. from *Puges* "for one little orchard?"[1]

Ambiguities compounded, it may seem, but in truth these muffled voices of lamentation are hardly less explicit than others in my sample. About motives, as a rule, they are surprisingly forthcoming, those of *Puges* and his pals. And what is unclear about the seizure from *Puges,* it turns out, is characteristically unclear. *Carbo de Fonte rubeo* said that Berenguer de Bleda took 33s. from him and that "then at once" Berenguera de Puigdàlber came and broke into

1. R1-3433.

Carbo's house on account of her "right" in those 33s.[2] Here the motive is quite as visible as the apparently procedural nature of the initial seizure is inexplicit, as is the interest of Berenguera—was it official or familial?—in the affair. At Caldes de Malavella a host of claims against Arnal de Perella was associated with pleas unspecified conducted in his name by men unidentified. Everywhere in these peasant habitats command, demand, and constraint are on the loose, stalking the contingencies of daily life without proclaiming their credentials. There was talk about right and wrong, about rights and their violation. There was talk about lords and about the property of lords, or lordship (*dominium, dominicatura*). There was little mention of functionaries by title, the way we might speak of policemen or Members of Parliament; no visible interest in spheres of competence; no talk about offices as such. What went unsaid, as taken for granted, was order, possession, and protection of possession.

An Order of Territorial Lordship

People were conscious of the Count or (after August 1162) of the King. Every memorial names him, one or the other, usually impersonally; six of them are explicitly addressed to the Count or the King. In the Llobregat domains one remembered the purchase of an honor "by the Count's order," and deplored attacks on the "Count's bailiff." This was the "Count's village," where Raimund Berenguer IV must often have been seen riding through with his entourage. The same was true of Caldes de Malavella, where the Lord-Count's travelling "family" would have broken their journeys to and from Occitania; and what preoccupied the author of our memorial about those places was the Count's habitual absence. Had the Count lingered or cared, it is implied, he would know that his service in the campaign against Muslim Almería had been ig-

2. F2-3141.

nored, his fields neglected. Few other domains were so convenient to his itineraries. Yet almost everywhere, even in remote villages like Esclet or Argençola, the losses were imputed to the Lord-Prince, were represented as usurpations. There may appear to have been some strategic design in this appeal to lordly interest, a way of seizing attention; but it is not really clear that the integrity of fiscal domains figured concretely in the questionnaire put to the localities. At Font-rubí "the Count who is our best lord" was himself charged with imposing uncustomary taxes. And there as elsewhere the appeal to the Count or King was affective and reflexive, on the theme our suffering is also yours.[3] Count Raimund Berenguer IV was *something like* the king his ancestors had once officially served. His peasant-tenants, like *P. Compan* at Font-rubí and *Amallus de Valoria* at Corró, can have had no trouble recognizing the Count's son who was, after August 1162, king as well as count. Nothing had changed in an order wherein tenancy and subjection were thoroughly confused.

For theory and ideology were at a minimum. People appealed to the Count's pleasure at Caldes and Llagostera, to his lordship at Font-rubí; everywhere to his nobility rather than to his office. That is why the men who judged and charged seem so autonomous, seem in the ominous shadows of distress less like agents than like lords themselves. Raimund de Ribes and Arnal de Perella were untitled purveyors of heavy-handed justice. Like the masters of castles almost everywhere else who are not called "castellan"—Guilelm de Sant Martí, Deusde, Pere de Bell-lloc—such men exercised the Count's or King's lordship without his nobility, substituting their pretensions for his diluted official presence.

No one doubted that the Lord-Prince had it in his power to remedy injustice. His peasants believed so, or perhaps in some cases were persuaded so by the scribes and others who questioned them. But it is far from clear that they had any personal experience of

3. F1-3409.

such exalted solicitude. The men who confronted them in streets
and fields or rapped on their doors were hardly the Count's men in
their view of things, nor was the justice they knew of so manifestly
that of the Count or King. The men at Font-rubí mentioned
"pleas" (*placita*) as occasions for "confirming right," that is, for
guaranteeing to attend or accept terms of judgment, or paying to be
free of such obligations.[4] At Caldes de Malavella *Poncius* the clerk
paid 30s. for daring to take the law in his own hands in a dispute
with his brother.

There was something insistently personal about these procedures
of constraint, seizure, and compensated acquittance. The scribes,
doubtless echoing their informants, refer to pleas also at Ribes and
Cabra; they seldom speak of justice as such. Nor of agency. Their
mention of *vikarios* at Font-rubí is pejoratively vague, while at
Cabra only the bailiff himself, Bertran de Vilafranca, refers to himself as a functionary. It is possible that bailiffs and men holding
powers of justice and command such as kings once delegated to
counts and vicars understood that they were sharing commended
jurisdictional rights, inconceivable that any distinction between re-
galian and lordly prerogative influenced their behavior. The scribe
who evoked official status by speaking of vicars at Font-rubí was
also the only one to mention a *ságo*—he figures in the service of
one of the armed oppressors, surely reminiscent of the Visigothic
saxo, a lesser officer of justice; here for once the ancient public
order found vestigial expression.[5] Yet there is nothing in the memorials and hardly more in other records of comital lordship to
suggest that the peasants and scribes thought of the Count's or
King's commended men, nor even the latter themselves, as an
administrative corps, let alone as a hierarchy.

Why should people have thought so? The power they experienced in their rural habitats was that of a lordly protectorate, not a

4. F2-3141.
5. F1-3409.

commonwealth. The appeal at Font-rubí was to "our natural lord."[6] Peasants could distinguish between their lords, doubtless finding remote lord-princes preferable to castellans, bailiffs, and their overbearing servants. It was harder to differentiate between lordships remote and immediate, even for those, like Berenguer Mir in the Gironès or Raimund de Ribes, who were imposing customary obligations on tenants to their own profit as well as the Lord-Count's. Who can doubt that at Terrats some bailiffs had lately attempted to collect from peasants beyond customary dues of hospitality? What can only be imagined is how those collectors justified their demands. Their power was their presence, attended by menacing servants; their participation in the constraints of territorial lordship; their arrogation of status. And it must always have been easier to admit their claims than resist them, to acquiesce in order to avoid lordly anger.

On the Threshold of Accountability

Such acquiescence in power was habitually unwritten. The masters who got it could not secure it save by the uneasy repetitions that created customs. Some of these new customs may have found their way into the fiscal surveys (*capbreus*) of comital and (later) royal domains, but these were by no means instruments of commended power. On the contrary, the very existence of such records fixing renders deemed to be the Lord-Prince's alone tended to inhibit the bailiffs and vicars in the peasants' favor. But the *capbreu* did little else to defend peasants from their daily masters in the villages. It was neither a privilege nor, politically speaking, a charter. It prescribed lordship only, representing rights of justice and banal powers indistinctly from patrimonial ones. And it left bailiffs and vicars free to account for their service as they saw fit, which is to say with just

6. F1-3409 dorse.

that measure of freedom they needed to encroach on the lordship they exploited and shared.

Until 1151, it appears. In that year the great survey compiled for old comital domains under the direction of Bertran de Castellet introduced a startling novelty. It prescribed not only the obligations of tenants in the Count's lordship but also the shares of bailiffs and vicars in that lordship. No fewer than fourteen of the seventeen constituent charters refer to these shares, almost always as "fiefs" (*feva*).[7] This marked a step toward accountable service in the Count's domains, which included six of the localities that rendered complaints in these and subsequent years; and since the memorials of five of these six places appear to antedate 1151, it looks as if Bertran's *capbreu* was a deliberate consequence of the inquiry. From then on bailiffs and vicars in these domains might be held responsible for their own shares in comital lordship as well as for the Count's share, that is, for excesses in their appointed fiefs. But the import of this apparent reform should not be overstated. There is no sign that the Count's servants in localities were yet required to account with any regularity. They remained the Count's commended men, their official status unstated, their fidelity taking precedence over their competence. Indeed, the importance of the survey-charters of 1151 in my present context is that they confirm the impression that these servants were affectively dependent by referring to the enfeoffments by which they were compensated. I do not wish to minimize the functional character of these feudal entitlements: the Count's scribes as well as one bailiff himself referred to vicars and bailiffs, as such, thereby signalling their quasi-official status. But the memorials of complaint are habitually inexplicit; the people closest to the reality of commended power had to be induced to see how such power differed from authority, to comprehend that the violent men about them were not so much their lords as they naturally seemed. It was the scribes who insinu-

7. *FAC,* ii, no. 1; i, ch. 2.

ated the idea of agency, who placed a new value on communication, inviting the appeal to authority that entailed some concept of responsibility.

The written word may already have had some role in communications between the Lord-Prince and his men in the localities. Bertran de Vilafranca mentions the King's *segels,* or sealed letters of direction, in the letter of his own that contains his grievances. Yet the memorials of complaint say nothing else about the literate engagement of lords and agents. People at Caldes de Malavella remembered that Arnal de Perella had been summoned to service, not how he had been summoned. The formal diversity of the memorials of complaint together with the singularity of the survey of 1151 suggests that these appeals for information were novel and irregular. Less still can the action of men with power in the villages have been a literate operation. There is nothing in the memorials to show that parchments were thrust before peasants, that their marks or subscriptions were required to validate or consent to judgments or transactions (such as those inscrutable sales of persons at Caldes and Llagostera, not one of which seems to have survived in writing). No doubt the people of our localities resorted to written forms of conveyance and sale as did free tenants everywhere in Catalonia in accordance with a written law not yet obsolete; yet for these enactments the scribes who drafted according to formularies need not have been much more lettered than the principals. Between peasants and the local masters they accused, the relation was customary rather than legal, a relationship of spoken words, of reminders, of threats often amounting to intimidation.[8]

Could that customary relationship be represented in writing? When the problem is put like this it can be seen that customs fell into two categories. On one hand were the agrarian dues and

8. On the place of writing in early Catalonia, see generally Bonnassie, *La Catalogne,* i, 192–195, 500–507; and Michel Zimmermann, "Ecrire et lire en Catalogne du IXe au XIIe siècle" (Paris, Thèse d'Etat, 1992).

renders well known to peasants and collectors alike, tending to be fixed and fixed surely at standard levels in some places, obligations set out in *capbreus*. On the other hand were the increments exacted by vicars and bailiffs or encroachments inflicted by them. The latter were necessarily unfixed, willful in their essence; unwritten and uneasy supplements, as it were, to the *capbreus*. It is safe to imagine that the local masters were content to leave them unwritten. But they were then at risk that peasants might see the discrepancy between the Lord-Prince's customs and their real obligations. In 1144 the peasants at Sant Pere d'Osor and neighboring vills purchased exemption not only from the Count's arbitrary tax (*forcia*) but also from that of the Count's men.[9] Of domains making complaint in the memorials, only Corró seems to have claimed enfranchised status; neither there nor in the other places have we the texts of charters that would prove the same measure of perspicacity as at Osor. Peasants in the old comital domains can hardly have expected a written accountancy of their vicars' and bailiffs' exactions because these functionaries were under no obligation even to the Lord-Prince to render written accounts.

This fact, however surprising it may seem, is fundamental to understanding the memorials of complaint. As late as about 1155 the only written accounts for the domains of the Lord-Count of Barcelona were the *capbreus* themselves; that is, static descriptions of rights over tenants and lands such as might serve to test the performance and declarations of bailiffs and vicars on their faith. This was an accountability of fidelity rather than of competence, enabling its subjects to keep silence about receipts unmentioned in the *capbreus*. It is likely that the survey of 1151 was preparatory to a more demanding supervision of the bailiffs, for soon thereafter audits for individual domains were being recorded in written forms that became regular in the 1170s. By that time the inquiries into the

9. *CPC*, i[1], no. 61.

deportment of functionaries had been in progress for many years, quite long enough to prove that tighter surveillance would not suffice to transform territorial lordship into administration.[10]

For little was done to ensure that bailiffs and vicars were accountable for their profits and increments of lordly power. But is it really likely that much was even attempted in this direction? This question brings me to the very nature of the memorials of complaint themselves. Were they not manifestly the records of a judicial campaign of administrative remedy? The best reason for thinking so is that the memorials have the form of judicial records. They were directed to the Count, as many of them explicitly say, and later to the King; two of them appeal specifically to the King's court or judgment.[11] Detailing complaints and allegations, they resemble the records formerly labeled *clamores* or *rancuras* such as were required to institute procedures at law in the old Pyrenean counties. What is more, the concentration of at least five of these memorials in the period c. 1145–1162 is consistent with other evidence that in these charged years during and after his great conquests, Count Raimund Berenguer IV sought to reestablish his authority by judicial means. The codification of the new territorial law of lordship and fiefs known as the *Usatges* of Barcelona as well as the convocation of numerous great pleas (*iudicia*) in the 1150s both attest to this initiative. Yet it is hard to find a link between these phenomena. Not a single one of the extant memorials of complaint can be traced in extant records of judgment during the half century after 1145. This silence may be significant; just as in the eleventh century it was surely easier to take depositions than to get them tried. Moreover, because the *iudicia* known to me are normally lacking their pertinent lists of complaints, it looks as if cases were intentionally preserved either as memorials of allegations or as judgments, but not as both. Someone made that selection,

10. *FAC*, i, chs. 2, 3.
11. Namely, R1-3433, R2-3217; see also F1-3409.

probably in the years 1178–1196. Nor does the verbal form of the complaints suggest a uniform campaign toward 1150. The five records antedating 1162 have no form in common, although it is possible that the expression "these are the complaints which the people of _____ make" which figures in the depositions of Terrassa was standard or became so. It is found after 1162 in the complaints of Font-rubí, Cabra, and Argençola, as well as in later ones for Molela, Igualada, and Tàrrega.[12]

Whatever their consequence, the memorials of complaint were judicial records, an appeal to the Lord-Count's immanent power of remedy. But it must have been unclear to any who read them what practical judgment could be rendered on such testimony. Trial in usual forms, solemn pleas, would have had to be held in the domains themselves, an unrealistic option that must have been ruled out at once. What was required was not so much judgments as audits of the vicars, castellans, and bailiffs; and while this distinction between modern forms of accountability would hardly have occurred to the twelfth-century people here in view, it usefully reminds us that the memorials of complaint were not only appeals to remote authority but also descriptions of local reality. They were, indeed, accounts. And they were accounts of precisely the sort routinely missing in the written review of commended lordship. They laid bare the relations between the Lord-Prince's men in the domains and his tenant-peasants. They rendered account of the inner sanctum of local delegated power: the occasions of justice, hospitality, and visible accumulated wealth. They went to the very structure of fiscal obligations and receipts. For example, the complaints of Terrassa (c. 1145–1150) consist chiefly of a list of alleged thefts by the castellan Deusde: 6s., 1 wether, and 2 pairs of chickens from *Petrus Guilelmi de Ruuira;* 15s. from *Carbonel de Font de Coloma;* 6 quarters of grain from *Guilelmus Gerouart;* and so on. The

12. *FAC,* i, 91–97; ACA, Cancelleria, pergamins extrainventaris 3148, 3493, 3514. For some judgments, see *DI,* iv, nos. 67, 71, 88, 98, 99, 114; *LFM,* i, no. 483; ACA, Cancelleria, perg. extrainv. 3133.

"brief of evils" inflicted on villagers at Caldes de Malavella and Llagostera (c. 1150) begins as a rhetorical account of the vicar's malfeasance before proceeding to itemize his alleged seizures and extortions. These records bear some resemblance to the earliest extant fiscal accounts for comital domains in Catalonia, which date from these very same years; and not accidentally so, for they appear to be the work of the same scribes, still mostly anonymous.

Indeed, it would be a mistake to distinguish categorically between surveys (*capbreus*), accounts of receipt and expenditure, and lists of complaints. Just as toward 1157–1158 the earliest surviving estates of annual account appear to be nothing other than the annotation of *capbreus*,[13] so I find complaints cast in the forms of capbreus or of acccounts (*computa*) or even of the two at once. The memorial of Caldes and Llagostera is explicitly a "brief of evils", as we have seen; but that of Valmala is an even more telling example of formal conflation. This record begins and ends as an inventory of land at Valmala held by Dorca from the Count. Still, it cannot have been made by Dorca or his men, for it begins by itemizing seizures from subtenants at *Pegeres*. Someone from the Count's entourage inquiring of tenants about their obligations had been told instead (or besides) about their payments. Even more clearly the "malefactions" of Berenguer Mir at Esclet and Ganix (c. 1152–1160) were recorded in a "commemoration" listing both obligations and seizures; that is, a record at once prescriptive and descriptive.

From this point of view it might seem that statements of seizure (*querimoniae*) as well as statements of account (*computa*) evolved from *capbreus,* and considered strictly as a matter of diplomatic that may be true. The *capbreu,* or inventory, was the old and fundamental if not even unique form of administrative account in Mediterranean societies; the assimilation to it of records of judicial complaint (*clamores*) cannot have been new in 1150. What *was* apparently new at that time was—to speak of an innovation of territorial lordship in

13. *FAC,* ii, no. 7.

our terms—the idea of administrative review, the idea that prescriptive accounts (such as *capbreus*) should be supplemented so as to
afford periodic statements of collection and balance by means of
which the ruler's courtiers could form better judgments of the
quality of service.

Now it looks as if lists of abusive seizures may have been among
the earliest such estates of account to be made; and if this is so I feel
entitled to wonder whether the more specific idea of recurrent
written accountancy may have arisen in Catalonia from the complaints of malfeasance in the Lord-Count's domains toward 1150.
Similarly in Occitania there is little evidence of seigneurial accounting in writing other than surveys before the famous inquiries
of King Louis IX in 1247–1248, which produced itemized accounts of seizures and extortions. In any case, the memorials of
complaint cannot be regarded as narrowly judicial, nor for that
matter is it safe to distinguish between "judicial" and "administrative" functions in these later years of Count Raimund Berenguer
IV. From his point of view the problem at that time was one of
lordship and service, of the fidelity of omnicompetent servants in
the domains; it was a problem of accountability.

In one respect, however, the memorials of complaint stand distinct from other accounts: they are accounts of violence. More
exactly, they are accounts of arbitrary behavior that typically lapsed
into violence or distraint. Their governing verbs are "to take"
(*tollere*), "take away" (or "steal," *abstulere, auferre*), "break (in)"
(*frangere*), "strike" (or "beat," *verberare*), "seize" (*rapere*), "eject" (*ei-
icere*), "lose" (*perdere*), and the like; these do not altogether displace
more neutral verbs, such as "give" (*donare*), "collect" (*colligere*), and
"hold" (*tenere*), but they impart so emphatically negative a tone to
the records that contain them that I cannot hope to make sense of
them in narrowly fiscal terms. The authors of these records were
usually claimants, not defendants. The people they charged would
surely have accounted differently, given the chance (that is, if capable at all of so bizarre an exercise!), yet not necessarily more accu-

rately.[14] They might have chosen other verbs to describe their settlements with peasants and collections from them. The real problem is to know where they would have drawn the line between "just" and "unjust." The memorials, while they hold some informative clues, do not suffice to solve that problem. They represent an imposed accountability bearing the official values of territorial lordship, not the accountability of the men and women who exerted power over *A. de Plano* at Gavà and *Guilelmus de Nogér* at Ribes and all the rest. These were the ones with power—they and their cronies—in the Lord-Prince's domains: Guilelm de Sant Martí at Gavà, Deusde at Terrassa, Arnal de Perella at Caldes and Llagostera, Berenguer Mir at Esclet and Ganix, Berenguer de Bleda at Font-rubí, Dorca at Valmala, Pere de Bell-lloc at Corró, Raimund de Ribes in the Ribes valley, Berenguer de Clariana at Cabra and Argençola, and Bertran de Vilafranca at Cabra. Only the last of these got in his innings. What would we give to hear them all! Only their victims created the portraits we have. Yet if the subjects would have rejected the art, they might nonetheless have recognized the likenesses.

Profiles of Exploitative Power

They loom large, oversized, in the memorials, these powerful ones. As they did among the people who knew them in the villages, who feared or resented them, who named them, individually, in all the complaints. Most of these alleged tormentors can be identified in other records as well, although seldom fully enough either to confirm or to invalidate the impressions conveyed by the complaints. Impressions, plural: it matters that these are diverse, even

14. Compare F3-3288: ". . . non solebamus dare quod .ii. qe. ordei per lozet et nunc faciunt nobis dare .iiii. qe . . ." with *FAC*, ii, no. 18: "Primum ad diem qua ego emparaui baiuliam Gerunde baiulus Gerunde non dabat domino comiti de lezdis et usaticis nisi .dccc. solidos et ego dono inde domino meo de ipsis lezdis et usaticis mille .d. solidos pro unoquoque anno."

though I must not fail to allow for the distorting influence of intermediary scribes more or less faithful to sentiment and animus. These impressions bring us close to the lived experience of power in these rural societies.

Guilelm de Sant Martí and Deusde were great lords of the Vallès and the Llobregat valley. Deusde was castellan at Terrassa when he was accused toward 1150 and perhaps had been so for many years. He held a benefice on the Count's revenues there, from which the bailiff had to pay him fifty pigs.[15] Guilelm had no such right at Gavà, although conceivably he had some claim to or had been deprived of such a right. His violence reads like that of an angry man. A favored companion of Count Raimund Berenguer IV, he had been party to a spectacular dispute between the Count and Guilelm Raimund of Montcada in the 1130s. It seemed for a moment that Guilelm de Sant Martí might secure the whole Montcada patrimony together with Guilelm Raimund's divorced wife Beatriu; in the end he settled for her in what proved to be a lasting and fruitful marriage. Their honorial lordships extended from the coastal lands west of the Llobregat eastward through the Vallès.[16]

15. CC, ii, 147; CSC, iii, nos. 938, 972, 974, 983, 984; FAC, no. 1Q; i, 171.

16. There is much confusion about this Guilelm de Sant Martí and his posterity; see Santiago Sobrequés i Vidal, Els barons de Catalunya (Barcelona, 1957), p. 64bis; CC, i, 414; iii, 782, 790; cf. ii, 190. The evidence seems to me to show that Guilelm married Beatriu as a young man, that their son Guilelm ceded rights in the castles of Montornès and Montbui to his wife Anglesa, that as late as 1172 the two Guilelms and their wives donated to Sant Viçenç de Pedrabona (Garraf); and that an oft-noted testament of August 1189 is not that of the elder Guilelm de Sant Martí but of his young grandson, who had a daughter and a pregnant wife, Alamanda, as he wrote, El "Libre Blanch" de Santas Creus (cartulario del siglo XII), ed. Federico Udina Martorell (Barcelona, 1947), no. 325. See also no. 133; CSC, iii, no. 920; LFM, i, nos. 295–307, 459; La baronia de la Conca d'Òdena, ed. María del Carmen Alvarez Márquez. Fundació Noguera. Textos i Documents, 25 (Barcelona, 1990), nos. 40, 44; L'arxiu antic de Santa Anna de Barcelona del 942 al 1200 (aproximació històrico-lingüística), ed. Jesús Alturo i Perucho, 3 vols. Fundació Noguera. Textos i Documents, 8–10 (Barcelona, 1985), iii, nos. 329, 432.

So the domains Guilelm was charged with violating lay in the center of his zone of interest. Whatever the provocation, his alleged distraints were as systematically violent as anything to be found in the memorials. He "broke into" the three clustered vills of the lower Llobregat plain, seized donkeys and pigs, imposed labor services, and helped himself to the Lord-Count's properties: a dove-cote, an orchard, and the forge at Sant Climent. His demands and seizures were abetted by men in his service, including his bailiffs, who beat *Arnallus Bunucii*'s and the Count's men when they refused to work on Guilelm's summons, broke into a house, and on one occasion threw a spear at a comital bailiff. The scribe evokes a perceived solidarity between Guilelm de Sant Martí and his men, switching the verbs from singular to plural forms and back: "He takes hospitalities in the Count's vills . . . and they stole sheep and goats" from people coming and going and then demanded redemption-payments for their return.

This is hardly the account of a raid. Guilelm has moved in on the Count's lordship in force, demanding maintenance for his knights, and importing his own bailiffs, who were recognized as such, to carry out his distraints. Making exception for a few violent incidents, what shocks here is the audacity of a lord-baron claiming the fullness of lordship in a comital domain where people believed he had no right. There is nothing to suggest any peculiar disposition to violence; even the beatings may be regarded as routine inducements to compliance. Guilelm may have pressed for some share in this lordship, notably hospitality, because of the convenience of the lower Llobregat to his itinerary. The exercise of coercive force came easily to Guilelm and his men. What cannot be known is whether his uncontested lordly power felt the same.

With Deusde there was no such problem of invasive disruption. He was entitled to command at Terrassa. Yet the Count's tenants there charged him with seizures so itemized as to create a reliable impression of his ordinary methods. Not content to accept his share of the customary rents from the bailiff nor that of the arbitrary

tallage (*chestes*), he imposed himself on the householders directly
and personally. He visited houses himself, doubtless with his men
looking on, demanding money and produce—sacks of grain,
lambs, pork-sides—and losing his temper when the people sometimes resisted. From the distribution of sums in coin it looks as if a
typical demand was around 6s. and 3 quarters or mitgers of grain
(*blad*); but since seizures amounting to 50s., 58s., and even 200s. are
reported, it would seem that Deusde returned repeatedly to some
victims. It was dangerous to oppose him, for he was in the habit of
beating people, and, worse, of striking them on the head. *Guilelmus
Gerouart* told of the seizure of 6 quarters of grain and a wether,
while his mother had a tooth knocked out. *Raimundus Uldrici* reported no theft but had his "head broken" (*fregit capud*); while
Raimundus de Canneto could not escape the same injury by paying
6s. From *Petrus Guilelmi de Brugera* Deusde took 3s. and 3 mitgers of
barley "and struck his wife."

Here if ever we seem to have a case of routine petty tyranny. It is
easy to imagine the Count's castellan descending on the tenants: he
gouges them, beats a few of them physically (*pour encourager les
autres?*), and provokes their itemized bill of damages. The psychic
profile of violence seems clear. Yet Deusde must have thought of
himself as a licensed protector. He shared in the lordship. He probably occupied the Count's "palace."[17] His visitations may have
been felt as raids but they left no collective memory as such. They
were repeated, accumulative acts of intimidating lordly power. In a
competitive habitat of aggrandizing castellans, Deusde found it hard
to content himself with customary shares in the fiscal lordship of a
growing domain at Terrassa.

The situations were similar at Corró, Font-rubí, and the Ribes
valley, as well as at Castellvell de Rosanes, a non-comital lordship.
In these places, too, castellans or vicars seem to have worked out of

---

17. On the comital buildings at Terrassa, see *CR*, xviii (1991), 288–289; and
FAC, i, 171.

neighboring castles to bully householding tenants and peasants. Yet the profiles of these men and their acts differ from those of Guilelm and Deusde and from one another. This was partly because the local circumstances, while similar, were not quite the same. Font-rubí was a developing habitat unlike the old Ribes, where Raimund de Ribes lived as virtually a viceroy. Pere de Bell-lloc had no customary share in the lordship of Lower Corró, unlike the vicars and castellans at Font-rubí and Ribes. But the memorials reveal differences of behavior that can only be attributed to personality. At Corró the charge against Pere de Bell-lloc was that he had broken into the Count-King's village, dragged men thence "often bound by the throat," and thrown them into prison. *Pages* joined with three other men of the place to list specific thefts in crops and animals from themselves and a neighbor. These allegations point not to routine exploitation but to a raid. Pere had no rights at Corró; but having been tempted or crossed he simply indulged himself some lucrative pillage. Yet for all I know such violence was recurrent at Corró, where several tiny parishes seem not to have had a bailiff of their own before the 1170s.

In the Ribes valley the problem was more nearly like that at Terrassa but on a larger scale. Our two sets of carefully itemized allegations are preoccupied with Raimund de Ribes, who held vicarial powers in the valley with its aggregated hamlets and who evidently doubled as bailiff as well. He had taken property and money from the people; mostly money, in sums higher than in the lowland domains, averaging perhaps over 25s. per individual. This fact may tell us as much about comparative wealth as about lordly constraint. But it relates quite exceptionally to circumstances of customary constraint mostly invisible elsewhere and is in keeping with the evidence of human character. Like Deusde at Terrassa, Raimund could be nasty when angered. When a kinsman of *Petrus Rastan* complained that Raimund had dispossessed *Petrus,* Raimund "struck him with spurs so that he did not get up from his bed until he died." "A peasant *Iohanes Oliba*" who was so indiscreet as to appeal to the King suffered a blow from Raimund "at the church portal." These were clearly acts of intimidation and the fact that they stand alone among some forty-eight reported incidents may suggest that most people had learned to keep out of Raimund's way. If that is so, *Petrus Faber* was foolish to complain to him that thieves had broken into his house: it cost him 8s.[18]

Raimund's was an orderly tyranny, marked more by greed than by violence. *Petrus Rastan* alleged that, having seized the manse of Roca corba, Raimund retained it in his own lordship, destroyed the King's mill there, and set up his own cloth mill from which he was collecting 30s. per annum. More than half the depositions tell of demands for money on occasions of intestacy, sterility, deaths or departures of children, or litigation of any sort. The peasants had no doubt that these demands were quite as wrongful as the seizures of land and animals: "these evils and many others" was the summation of their complaints by the people of Queralbs. It is not so clear, as we shall see, that they thought their vicar's deeds were unjust. But of Raimund's character or style apart from the reported demands and seizures the picture that develops is not that of a plunderer but of a magnate-entrepreneur far from the Lord-King's scrutiny remorselessly exploiting his jurisdiction over custom.[19]

At Font-rubí the situation was more complicated. Here it looks as if the Count's bailiffs were bold enough to share in the attempt of local magnates to expand their dominations at the expense of free peasants, not strong enough to hold that expansion within tolerable limits. In their first complaint, the people of Font-rubí charged that Raimund Berenguer IV himself ("our best lord") had imposed novel exactions and "quests" in barley, wheat, and money. But already the main complaints are reserved for the "vicars": that is, lords of the neighborhood claiming to exercise comital rights of justice, of whom the "lady-lord" (*domina*) of Mediona, Raimund

18. Both items in R1-3433.
19. R1-3433, R2-3217.

de Barbera, and Berenguer de Bleda are alleged to have helped themselves willfully to 20s. apiece as well as to "great forced exactions and gouges" in grain, animals, and wine. Amongst these lords Berenguer seems to be the chief culprit, and in two further memorials after 1162 he figures as a high-handed magnate preying on peasants through his castellans.[20]

The accusations against Berenguer and his cronies and castellans are more personal and less detailed than those against Deusde, Pere de Bell-lloc, and Raimund de Ribes. They are specific, to be sure. Berenguer's man Pere dels Archs "made great *forces* and great tolts on us, he has broken into our houses and stolen pigs and ham-sides and chickens and has broken our casks and he has taken chickens and gardens and trees and cheeses and eggs . . . [etc.]." But the damages are not itemized, at least not at first. The trouble had happened so fast (and perhaps so continuously) that the victims could do little better than wring their hands. Yet already in their first account comes the report of "another time in the month of August" when Berenguer de Bleda robbed *Raimundus Marti* and his brother-in-law *Berengarius* of an ox and one sextar of barley, and further attemps at itemizing damages follow. The memorial also includes other distinct grievances: against Berenguer de Mediona for taking "our donkeys . . . to his houses"; or "another time" for demanding carting-service to Tortosa. But these complaints tend to lose specificity and finally lapse into generalities: "we complain of Raimund de Barbera for the injury he has done." Seven other such charges follow.

In short, there is some formal ambiguity in the representation of grievance at Font-rubí. One reason for this must be that the scribes, or at least the first one, and perhaps also their informants, were more interested than those elsewhere in the character of their masters' misdeeds. Thus they not only reiterated generalities about forcible seizure and housebreaking, they recalled repeatedly that

20. F1–3409.

Berenguer de Bleda or his men "cut our beards." This at least was more subtle intimidation than Deusde's head-cracking at Terrassa. But they whacked people at Font-rubí, too. Nor is this all. Pere dels Archs has "now once again" seized "our donkeys" to assist in works of fortification for Berenguer. In subsequent memorials we are shown Berenguer de Bleda and his castellans imposing unprecedented maintenance (*albergae*) on the villagers "which he receives with all his *familia* and spends in his houses as he wishes." *Martinus de Fonterubeo* was conspicuously victimized. He complained "that B. de Bleda came into his house with all his family, Christians as well as Saracens, dogs as well as [other] animals, and he did this by great force and against *Martinus*'s will . and he built a stone oven there and he stayed there with all his family for five weeks . and occupied his upper houses and *Martinus* and his family stayed below." Yet another deposition had it that Berenguer de Bleda "sends his deputy with his donkey through their cellars" where he helps himself "to as much wine as he wishes against the will of those men."[21]

This is a different and sharper profile. Berenguer de Bleda is not loathe to exploit his jurisdictional powers: here as in the Ribes Valley and Gironès there is mention of judicial exactions. But Berenguer is more visible than Raimund de Ribes, more imposing,—and more pretentious. We can visualize him—him and his knights—clanking about the vills of Font-rubí, demanding provisions according to the military custom so common in Occitania and Catalonia. We can see him with his dependents and servants, including Muslim slaves perhaps acquired after the late conquests of Tortosa and Lleida, requisitioning rooms in a prosperous villager's quarters. And if I could surely connect the works of fortification for which donkeys were seized with this unwilling hospitality we might infer that Berenguer was promoting himself at the expense of men more nearly of his own status than he would have wished to

21. F2-3141, F3-3288.

admit. There are two other hints that this inference may be correct. One is that Berenguer is alleged to have borrowed (and abused) a mare for threshing his grain, as if he himself engaged in such rustic labor. The other hint is that *Martinus de Fonterubeo* "sustained great shame and great dishonor in his houses" for having been forced to lodge Berenguer and his entourage. Was this not the shame of being humiliated by the power and pretense of a peer?[22]

The troubles at Cabra and Argençola toward 1160–1175 reveal yet another ominous presence from over the hills. Berenguer de Clariana, swooping down "with his horsemen" to plunder the Lord-King's "palace" at Cabra, could not let other lords' tenants alone. At Argençola it was Berenguer de Aguiló, the other Berenguer's neighbor, who complained to the King on behalf of his villagers. But the detailed inventory of their alleged losses is not such as to prove that the lord of Clariana had raided them; if anything the spare allusions to tiresome oppression, inducing *Berengarius Maria* to abandon his tenement at Argençola, suggests that Clariana had been encroaching on Berenguer de Aguiló's lordship.[23]

And this is exactly what is visible in the more informative memorials from Cabra. There, it will be remembered, the old bailiff Bertran de Vilafranca charged Berenguer de Clariana and others with a variety of oppressive seizures, only to be charged himself by Berenguer and Guilelm de Concabella. It is not easy to reconcile these accounts. Bertran said that Bernard de Concabella, yet another alleged malefactor, had thrown *Arnal de Muntfred* in prison and exacted a ransom of 300s. to free him. Berenguer and Guilelm de Concabella charged that Bertran had ousted *Arnal* from his honor and driven him out of Cabra. Both charges could well be truthful. *Arnal de Muntfred* may be one of my few subjects who was

22. F1-3(3409, 3141, 3288). On honor and shame, see Chapter IV.
23. A3145.

demonstrably inept, or even vicious, as well as unlucky, falling afoul of menacing men in conflict with one another and in need of allies. Dare I imagine that *Arnal* rejected all dominations save the Lord-King's? This is not inconceivable, but as so often the voice sounding through the allegations is suppressed. What is clear is that Berenguer de Clariana and others had pretended to share in the fiscal jurisdiction that the King's bailiff could reasonably expect to exercise himself. Berenguer allegedly appropriated renders from the royal domain, he drew on "pleas" diversely involving the "people" of Tarragona and Cabra, and so on. Despite a royal directive to desist from forced demands, he compelled "your man" *Poncius de Barbera* to pay 60s. in recognition of his jurisdiction. As to Berenguer's motive, Bertran de Vilafranca leaves nothing to be imagined. He says that Berenguer forcibly appropriated domain lands next to Cabra village and downhill from Santa Maria de Pla, and that he and Bernard de Concabella had turned properties (*onore*) of the people of Cabra into "lordship [*dominicatura*] which they have given to knights."[24]

These observations say more about the designs of the powerful than about their style and methods. But what was only implicit in the lower Llobregat domains here comes starkly into view: a bailiff's vain struggles against ambitious rivals for shares in the King's lordship at Cabra. To the villagers—to *Poncius de Barbera* and *Pere de Turc* amongst others, not to mention the hapless *Arnal de Muntfred*—it can hardly have mattered much whose demands rained down on them. Given to seizures of produce and money, often in ways linked to judicial procedure as elsewhere, Berenguer de Clariana and the other magnates constrained people to obedience more by shows of force than by violence. Berenguer "and his horsemen" are brilliantly evoked not only as they "broke into" the King's palace—in Bertran's words this was virtually a desecration—

24. Ca1-2609.

but also as intimidating might preventing people from appealing "to you [Lord-King] for fear of those horsemen," who are so near when you are so far. What is new in the scene at Cabra is evidence that Bailiff Bertran was none too gentle himself in his ways. His accusers' memorial may seem untrustworthy on its face, coming from the very men charged by Bertran. Yet they had taken care to associate the "good men of Cabra" in their allegations, which were composed with singular clarity, and which seem in no way implausible. Their primary complaints had to do with forcible ousters from tenancies, arrests, and threats of violence; and by this testimony Bertran was himself guilty of the very sort of seizures and ransoms he himself had alleged. In short, Bertran would seem to have shared in a pattern of overbearing deportment, not so much afflictive as intimidating; the exercise of command, demand, and distraint. And what is further implied in the particulars against him is that one could not hope to secure submission at Cabra without retainers or allies. If Bertran had to expropriate enemy peasants, it was surely to reward his friends.[25]

* * *

It is time to revisit Caldes de Malavella and Llagostera, where toward 1150 was produced the most sharply drawn portrait in my rural gallery. Here for once the scribe, or more likely the anonymous individual who collected and dictated the complaints against Arnal de Perella, was capable of unequivocal and differentiated recollections. His memorial includes perfectly itemized lists of exactions and extortions dating back to the Count's expedition to Almería (1147), moving forward in time, and distinguishing between plaintiffs at Caldes and Llagostera. It was at Caldes that *Maria Guitarda* lost a 3-shilling pig; at Llagostera that Arnal "had" from *Archimballus* 8s., from *Dalmacius Conilii* 9s., and so on, before

25. Ca2-3474.

throwing them out of the village along with more than a dozen others. From these lists alone may be projected a plausible portrait. Like Raimund de Ribes a few years later Arnal was a manipulator of justice. His favorite technique seems to have been to sell his peace or quittance. *Raimundus Dominici* and *Geralla* figured out that "counting all occasions of money from pleas," Arnal de Perella had taken 25s. from them. *Guilelmus Suniarii, Bernardus Chabeca, Guilelmus Dalmacii, Petrus Poncii,* and *Raimundus Petri de Uilar* accounted for another 30s. (or 6s. apiece on average, the value of two pigs); *Raimundus Poncii* 3(s.), "*Stephanus* likewise. from *Martinus* 2. from *Petrus de Puig Besen* 10." Some nineteen men and women paid an average 5s. 10d. for such quittances. A bargain perhaps? One could deal with Arnal de Perella. There is no indication of afflictive constraint, such as at Terrassa, Ribes, and Font-rubí. But Arnal could extort for other reasons, and in larger average amounts, or for no reason at all. *Vital* knew that, for Arnal twice dunned him for money "and another time [took] one premium coverlet." No less characteristic was Arnal's manipulation of petty credit. If *Petrus Amallus*'s wife lost something of her freedom when someone else paid Arnal the 10s. she owed him, I think it likely that many others of the "sold" men and women here listed were in some sense lessened in status or stigmatized; by recording them as such the scribe bore witness to an intimidating local presence.[26] Armed servants were part of it. "Arnal de Perella's wife had 25s. from *Amallus Chapel* when the Count was on the expedition of Montpellier."

So much then from the lists alone. They reveal a local strong man exploiting justice and personal wealth, imposing himself officially while not failing to enrich himself. But we know much more than this about Arnal de Perella, because his accuser saw fit to preface his lists with a general account of his transgressions. The gist of this account is as follows: Arnal collects from the Count's "peasants great amounts of wheat and barley and other grains which he

26. On the problem of "sold" men and women, see above, p. 39.

spends in his house with his *familia* and his friends and his elders and relatives." He feigned illness when the Lord-Count summoned him to the expedition of Almería, putting the proceeds (for that purpose) to his own use, "and so he does every year . . . And it is a great injury to the Lord-Count and his peasants!" He neglects the Count's demesnes, so that instead of having surpluses in wheat, barley, feedgrain, and millet such as his predecessor Raimund Guilelm achieved, he squanders all on himself. "And it is a great injury to the Lord-Count!" He abuses the vintage, sending forth "from his house . . . two bachelors" who go through the peasants' vines when the grapes are newly ripe and return with filled baskets; he also took portions from vineyards where the churches of Santa Maria and Sant Esteve had tithes, making "therewith new wine which he drinks with his *familia;* and when all the vintage was in he would make a select white wine which "he drinks faithfully [*fideliter*] with his friends and elders and relations, except when the Lord Count's *familia* happens to stop there and drinks." Arnal also makes and consumes good red wine, although Raimund Guilelm used to trade it for feedgrain. And while Raimund used to pay the Count from a healthy surplus in coined money up to "250s. or 200 or 100" Arnal "doesn't give our Lord Count a single penny!" He has diverted the Lord-Count's judicial revenues—"all the revenues . . . from pleas of sold men and women"—and much else owed to the Count to his own uses. He has squandered the tenants' dues in pigs, spending two years' worth in one. Finally, he has driven out the old bailiffs and replaced them with his cronies, one of whom was (so to speak—the memorial is brilliantly explicit at this point) not up to the job. He entered into sworn pacts of fidelity with some men of Caldes, then broke his oaths, thereby precipitating disorders in which the young men of the villages were forced to flee "to the other honors of noble knights where they get on better."

This account, here considerably pruned of its declamatory rhetoric, renders Arnal de Perella more fully human in his failings than any of his contemporary functionaries in twelfth-century Catalonia. In fact, the account is so good that it poses a problem of perspective touched on already in Chapter I. It is hard to disengage Arnal and his doings from the opprobrium of their representation. Worsened by their perceived consequences, deeds are run together with perceptions. But *this is just how people must have experienced power* in the manses of Caldes and Llagostera. Not only the distraints but also the arrogant satisfactions of Arnal and his men were afflictions, subjects of complaint. For the accountant's point of view is more nearly "administrative" than that of plaintiffs elsewhere, directed not only to what the villagers have lost but also to what the Count has lost through Arnal's infidelity and incompetence. Yet if lost revenues matter more than physical abuse to this observer, that does not prove that Arnal de Perella was less violent than Deusde or Pere de Bell-lloc. It does prove that Arnal's ends were thought quite as interesting—and appalling—as his means. The charges are not so different, after all, from those at Font-rubí. Berenguer de Bleda may seem horsier than Arnal de Perella; both look rather like peasants on the make. And here again the "lifestyle" of a petty magnate seems on view. But the representation of these charges is different: the depictions are clearer than at Font-rubí; moreover, being narratively linked, they arrive at something like stereoscopic clarity.

The most vivid image in the complaints at Caldes and Llagostera is that of Arnal de Perella seizing from peasants and retiring to his house to eat and drink with his *familia.* They drink *fideliter,* but not it seems to the Count's health! The fidelities that interest Arnal are the ones he is imposing on his cronies and bailiffs—*his* bailiffs, I mean, not the Count's; he has a swelling clientele of dependents. Among these was a peasant named *Bernardus Vives,* who replaced one of the two bailiffs Arnal is said to have ousted. For him was reserved the memorialist's choicest invective: *Bernardus* "was then [when appointed] poor and now is rich. and he is a good accuser of wretched people. and he does many evil things in the land with his lord Arnal." As for *Arnallus Granelli,* Arnal's other bailiff, all that is said is that he began "rich. and is now a pauper." It looks as if official service did not pay. Arnal de Perella was a lord, in short, and one could prosper in his service.

And what made this intolerable is that Arnal was no lord to begin with! Chosen to supervise the Count's bailiffs and to exercise vicarial jurisdiction, he had received certain manses and revenues in fief from the Count; but it is clear that Arnal worked or supervised the working of the Count's demesne lands himself or was expected to do so. Yet the fields he tended, "with one pair of oxen," it was alleged, "were not enough for his dogs!" So there he is, this vicar (as he was called in the survey of 1151) entrusted with Count Raimund's lordship in a major agrarian domain, neglecting the Count's reserve farms, squeezing the tenants beyond customary renders, well served by a brutal bailiff exploiting justice for profit, and retreating to his house to live like a lord. To "live it up," as we might say, drinking with his *familia:* our narrative reiterates this detail. Arnal de Perella has no castle,[27] let me add, but that may come next. He is, in short, rather a fraud. One might perhaps put up with such bullying and strutting from a noble or even a knight, but hardly from a peasant. The evidence of such behavior is original in that it represents not merely event and consequence but also process: the process of social ascent. What our anonymous accuser has wrought is a description of the ways in which a new lordship was created: one of the least visible, possibly most frequent, and often most terrible occurrences in medieval history.[28]

27. This is a problematic point. The Roman towers, perhaps then in ruins, are never mentioned. There may have been some fortification on the hillock of Sant Maurizi 2.5 km. south of Caldes, for there is mention of a castle of "Malavela" in 1057 or 1058, *LFM,* i, no. 448. But there is no further known reference to this castle until after 1300, *CR,* v (1991), 293; while the memorial speaks only and repeatedly of Arnal's "house" (*domus sua*). See also *LFM,* i, no. 400.

28. The process could be more benign, it is true. Professor R. H. Hilton drew my attention to the story of Ketelbern of Canley whose successors "arrogated to themselves the lordship of Canley hamlet," *The Stoneleigh Leger Book,* ed. R. H. Hilton (Oxford, 1960), pp. xxxiv–xxxv, 30–35.

* * *

Was not Arnal's ambition that of all the men and women with power over the Lord-Prince's peasants? The temptation to seize or encroach on lordship seems to have been a constant factor in these local situations. And we might be pardoned for supposing from our outlook in a vastly different world that such ambitions and temptations molded a type of manipulative power; that Arnal de Perella was simply a better drawn copy from the model represented also by Guilelm de Sant Martí, Raimund de Ribes, and the rest. But that would be to lose sight of the deeper lesson of the memorials: that for all their expressive frailty the peasants and scribes recognized traits of command and coercion that enable us to differentiate their predicaments. Deusde's cranky head-cracking at Terrassa looks quite unlike Raimund de Ribes' cynical manipulation of custom in his valley; yet neither had need of the predatory ways of Pere de Bell-lloc or Berenguer de Clariana. Two further examples will complete the tour. In vills and manses adjoining Llagostera, Berenguer Mir was accused of "making great houses and plants [*plantas*] and farms" as well as usurping rents and services at Count Raimund's expense. He looks like a lesser Arnal de Perella, whom he may indeed have known, and even imitated. No afflictive violence is mentioned, simply the aggressive—and "unjust"—manipulation of tenures and revenues. On the other hand, the castellan Berenguer de Castellvell de Rosanes resembles Deusde and Berenguer de Bleda more than Arnal de Perella, perhaps not accidentally given the location of Castellvell between Terrassa and Font-rubí in the upper Llobregat valley. Struggling in the 1150s to free his customary lordship from an appointed dependence on Guilelm Raimund de Castellvell, Berenguer was charged by his lord with seizures and imprisonments, expropriations, and forced exactions and, like Deusde, with singularly intimidating threats and violence. He made a specialty with women. He seized and ransomed one woman—her name is not given—for all she was worth, cut off another's nose, and threatened other "men and women" of the lordship to blind them or amputate their noses, and even carried out such violence in sight of his lord's "lady" (*domina*).[29]

It bears repeating that the memorials are accounts of violence. They represent willful behavior, saying nothing about routinely acceptable benevolence toward people—except insofar as acts of will were deemed acceptable. (This may prove a considerable exception.) Nor can the violence as represented always be regarded strictly a phenomenon of lordship. Some of the outrages listed in the memorial of Castellvell may have been incidents of the war between Guilelm de Castellvell and his insubordinate castellan. The same caution applies to the memorials from Corró and Cabra. The memorials of complaint are partial and problematic evidence of the exercise of power in the rural domains that produced them. They are—and this, too, bears repeating—the only evidence we have.

The Nostalgia of Associative Lament

For the sake of clarity these depictions of exploitative power have been dealt with as if they were objective representations. My purpose has been to discover what kinds of behavior may safely be attributed to the subjects of complaint on the basis of manifestly partial evidence. But the results of this inquiry cannot be understood out of context. The difficulty lies not so much in the distortions or exaggerations of individual charges—these faults alone would hardly affect a typology based on the charges—as in the peculiarly subjective commentary that attends the charges and gives them their meaning. Here can be overheard an insistent voice of the countrysides telling of the traditions and ideals of village life.

29. Cast3509; cf. Garí, *El linaje de los Castellvell*, pp. 170–173; Salrach, "Agressions senyorials," p. 21.

It is a deliberately muted voice, to be sure. When the depositions were collected and recorded the scribes were inclined to represent them in the third person as (for instance) seizures by A from B. This seems to have been the prevailing form, deriving perhaps from the impersonal usage of *capbreus*. The complaints of Terrassa are entirely in a third-person voice; so are those of Gavà and Caldes-Llagostera, although in the latter case the texture is deceptive. In the memorial of Valmala and in one each of those from Font-rubí and Ribes departures from objective discourse look like lapses from a habitually descriptive mode.

But in other records the subjective intrusions can no longer be called lapses. One of the later memorials of Font-rubí begins correctly enough before slipping irreversibly into first-person plural forms that seem to reveal the scribe sharing the grievances he is writing, a circumstance even more evident in the impassioned complaints which form the earliest record from that place. And I recall that in the Ribes valley the same scribe who wrote descriptively in one parchment reported depositions in another as if the victims themselves were speaking: compare "R. de Ribes took one cow away from *Petrus Rastan de Ribes*" with "R. de Ribes took 20s. away from me *Berengarius Bonifilii*."[30] At Corró, where another scribe appears at first to have reserved a formal objectivity, the complaint of "[us] *Pages* and *A. de Valoria* and *G. Iohanis* and *P. de Valoria* to our Lord-King" bursts through as a fully subjective declaration on the part of themselves "and all other free men [*franchearii*] . . . who are your own men."

These tendencies to subjective expression were far from accidental. No scribal convention could contain the vehemence with which these villagers felt their grievances nor were they content to leave it to others to address their ruler. "Lord Count Raimund Berenguer," cried the people of Font-rubí, "all these evils that are

---

30. F3-3288, R1-3433, R2-3217.

written in this charter are pillages and sorrows and *forces* and tolts
that Raimund de Barbera and Berenguer de Bleda and Pere Bernard de Puigdàlber and the Lady of Mediona and their men have
inflicted on us. And Oh Lord Count, if you will not give us redress,
tell us so, that we may go on our way!"[31] The threat of exodus
resounds also in the apostrophic lament at Ribes: "May the Lord
King know that the things we have reported are true . and we shall
bring [them] to truth in his court by judgment or oath . and if he
does not accept another counsel about us . we are all exiles!"[32]
People felt for one another in these outcries. Nor were these idle
threats. The memorials of Esclet-Ganix, Cabra, and Argençola as
well as that of Ribes just quoted refer to derelict manses or tenements. At Argençola, where the losses suffered by *Berengarius Maria*
could not be fully accounted because he had left his family and
gone away, three other "companions" had also lost property and
fled to "another land . and now we don't know where they are nor
what they lost . but we know that they lost all they possessed." And
of Caldes de Malavella and Llagostera it was asserted that its best
young people were escaping "to the other honors of noble knights
where they get on better." These are the words of desperate people
reaching out for each other.

A collective desperation, that is,—yes, but let us not misread the
urgency in their words. The peasants of Caldes, Font-rubí, Ribes,
and Argençola were first of all crying out to their Lord-Prince. He
was for them the visionary deliverer; they could fall back on the
threat of exodus (if not the reality) as other Catalans were wont to

31. F1-3409: "Domine Raimundi Berengarii comes, omnia hec mala que in
ista karta scribuntur sunt rapine et gemitus et forces et toltes que Raimundus de
Barbera et Berengarius de Bleda et Petrus Bernardi de Podio albari et domina de
Midiona et suis homin[e]s . quas faciunt nobis . et ó domine comes si non feceris
ad nos redergér discite ad nos, ut eamus nostram uiam."

32. R1-3433: "Sciat dominus rex quod hec que diximus uera sunt et ad
ueritatem ducemus in curia ipsius uel iudicio uel sacramento et nisi acceperit aliud
consilium de nobis omnes sumus exules." See further to this effect C-Ll-2501,
quoted on p. 100.

do.[33] But they were acting in submission rather than association (still less rebellion). Lordship, not community, is what has suffered injury from oppressive behavior, threatening the affective adjustment which held people in fidelity to the Count or King. That is why some scribes had trouble holding to a traditionally descriptive mode of narration in face of emotional eruptions; the inherent orality of lordship burst through the literate formality of an official diplomatic in some of the memorials, notably those of Font-rubí, Corró, Ribes, Cabra, and Argençola. People could suffer a remotely officious reality of lord-rulership so long as they felt secure in such submission: that was, indeed, the venerable old way; failing such assurance they had to reanimate a humanely affective dependence.

So they reached also for each other. They acted associatively, without yet quite uniting as communities. This is the significance of the first- and third-person plural verbs that resound in their memorials. "These are the complaints that the people of Terrassa make to the Count of Barcelona." At Lower Corró the four named plaintiffs identify with "all the other free men likewise who [we] are your men." In the memorials of Ribes, where complaints are listed individually, the apostrophes are poignantly collective: "these evils and many others did R. de Ribes to us men of Queralbs." The lordly interest is part of this vulnerable solidarity: "the men of Queralbs tell you, Lord King, that you are losing your share in barley-threshing in Queralbs and in Fustanyà and in Pardines and in Ribes and in Batet."[34] At Font-rubí the earliest memorial of com-

33. See also *FAC,* ii, no. 131; and generally E. R. Wolf, "On Peasant Rebellions," *Peasants and Peasant Societies: Selected Readings,* ed. Teodor Shanin (Harmondsworth, 1971), pp. 272–273. For parallels in other societies, see Jerome Blum, *Lord and Peasant in Russia from the Ninth to the Nineteenth Century* (Princeton, 1961), pp. 106–113, 163, 266–268; E. F. Irschick, "Peasant Survival Strategies and Rehearsal for Rebellion in Eighteenth-Century South India," *Peasant Studies,* ix (1982). 232–238; and James C. Scott, *The Moral Economy of the Peasant: Rebellion and Subsistence in Southeast Asia* (New Haven, 1976), intro. and ch. 7.

34. R2-3217.

plaints is cast almost entirely in impassioned first-person-plural language; and all four extant memorials (including a mostly illegible one) are from the associated people (*homines*) of Font-rubí. The "good men of Cabra" joined—or were claimed by?—Guilelm de Concabella and Berenguer de Clariana in charges against the bailiff Bertran de Vilafranca toward 1175.[35] Even at Caldes and Llagostera, where the representation of grievances eschews subjective verbiage, the sense of collective outrage comes through; here, indeed, more nearly an idea of community; and here again it is the Count and the peasants alike, and together, who suffer "great injury" from Arnal de Perella's seizures. Moreover, this community is evoked in uniquely affective terms. After Arnal made and broke his pacts

> never has the land done anything but get worse and to be battered by lightning, rocks, and hail and bad storms . and there is not even one-half of the men whom he found in that village when their troubles began. Between Caldes and Llagostera there used to be a hundred young men [*iuuenes*], counting the sons of peasants, also weavers and other notables [*magistri*] and bachelors who had money and grain. And they would lend to their lords and parents and neighbors . and now there is not a single one left who has anything of value . but they flee to the other honors of noble knights where they get on better. Again, if it would please the Lord Count to restore the bailiwicks to his old bailiffs it would be to his great profit. For if he does not, that will be his great injury.[36]

35. Ca2-3474.

36. C-Ll-2501: "Post quam hec sacramenta fuerunt facta et non obseruata . nunquam fecit terra nisi peiorare et fulminari lapidibus atque grandinibus et malis nebulis . et non est ibi medietas hominum quos inuenit in uilla illa quando malos eorum uenit super eos. Erant inter Kalidas et Lacustariam .c. iuuenes . inter filios rusticorum et testores . et alios magistros . et baculares qui habebant denarios . et annonam. Et acomodabant inde senioribus . atque genitoribus . et uicinis . et modo non est ibi unus solus qui habet aliquid boni . sed fugiunt in alios honores nobilium militum ubi melius se habent. . . . ."

Through the searing demoralization of their society these villagers clung to the vision of a better past. In fact, they were trying to
restore an old regime. That was explicitly the theme of the nostal-
gic early memorial of Font-rubí:

> First, the people of Font-rubí complain of the Count who is our best
> lord . of the usages that he has imposed on us that we never had in
> his father's lifetime . . . and we ask you [Raimund Berenguer IV] by
> God and by His Mother because you are our best lord that you
> restore to us the usages that your father and your grandfather had on
> us . and what we give you will be a great joy to you and if you
> cannot do [this, at least] put us in your demesne and keep us
> [there].[37]

In this place as at Caldes and Llagostera, and in different ways at
Gavà and Corró as well, the peasants see intruders staking out
positions between the Lord-Count and his tenants.

But on one point there was a difference. There were still—as late
as the 1150s—no castles at Caldes and Llagostera, and no castellans.
It is altogether likely that these were traditional franchisal communities such as had anciently flourished in a public order protected
by the counts in fortified cities. In most places such settlements had
been denatured, their communities fractured by the pressures of
banal lordship since the early eleventh century. At Font-rubí comital tenants had lived under the protection of castellans who had
respected franchisal custom until the 1140s, when ambitious new
magnates nurtured as knights and holding local fiefs and vicarial
rights upset an old order dating back to the days of Raimund
Berenguer I (1035–1076), if not to the founding of the old frontier

37. F1-3409: "Conqueritur homines de Fonte rubea. Inprimis de ipsum
comite qui est nostrum seniorem meliorem de usaticos que abet missos super nos
que non abemus unquam in uita de suum pater . . . & rogamus uos per deum et
per sua mater quare uos estis nostrum meliore seniorem quomodo tornetis nobis
in ipsos usaticos que tenuerint nobis pater uester et auium uestrum . et hoc quod
damus uobis magnum erit uobis gaudium et si non potueritis facere mitatis in
uestrum dominicum et retinetis nobis. . . ."

in the tenth century.[38] The new castellans or vicars were the problem, so that communities of free tenants could only place their
hopes in bailiffs (or former bailiffs, who may themselves have initi-
ated the complaints at Caldes-Llagostera and at Terrassa). At Terrassa, however, the record is too reticent to make clear whether a
preexistent sense of community was felt to be endangered. At
Corró the *franchearii* were certainly a community—more exactly, a
double community comprising the parishes of Santa Eulàlia of
High Corró and Sant Mamet of Lower Corró—when Pere de
Bell-lloc descended on them, presumably from his castle a few
kilometers to the east.[39] It is harder to discern traditional solidarities
in the frontier settlements at Cabra and Argençola.

Of all these domains it looks as if Caldes de Malavella and
Llagostera had the best preserved communities when their troubles
began. They were, accordingly, the most outrageously disrupted
places. For these people seizures, uncustomary demands, and pil-
laging were simply wrong—they were "evils" (*mala*) to be denounced and remedied. And since the remedy sought was judicial,
these wrongs may also have been thought unjust. Yet there are
signs that the equivalence between "wrong" and "unjust" was becoming problematic. Even at Caldes a fair number of seizures seem
to have been connected with judicial proceedings, while at Font-
rubí the repeated references to unexcused seizures may conceal
jurisdictional payments, fines, and the like. The most illuminating
case is that of Ribes.

The survival of franchisal communities in the Ribes valley was
probably more tenuous than elsewhere. Raimund de Ribes was
exercising practically unlimited powers as castellan-vicar, having

38. Bonnassie, *La Catalogne*, i, 243–260; *FAC*, i, 207; Pierre Bonnassie and
Pierre Guichard, "Les communautés rurales en Catalogne et dans le pays valencien
(IXe—milieu XIVe siècle)," *Flaran*, iv (1982), 79–85; reprinted in Pierre Bonnassie, *From Slavery to Feudalism in South-Western Europe*, trans. Jean Birrell (Cambridge, 1991), ch. 8.

39. Co3214; *FAC*, i, 169; ii, no. 14; and for Pere de Bell-lloc, *CC*, ii, 259–263.

apparently succeeded Gauceran de Sales, to whom in 1140 Raimund Berenguer IV had commended "the castle of Ribes and all strongholds in the whole valley of Ribes."[40] And the peasants who, one by one, alleged that Raimund had "taken away" from them had no doubt that he had injured them; "these evils" was the summation for Queralbs, and both their lists are allegations of malfeasance in pure and unrelieved form. But what is striking about *their* account is that when—as I have to suppose—they were pressed for reasons for the takings or seizures they reported, they were all too ready to supply reasons. "R. de Ribes took away 14s. from *Pere Miró* on account of his young son's dispute with another boy." "R. de Ribes took from me *Berengarius Bonifilii* 20s. . . . *because* I had two cows from a certain sterile woman who had died . . . Another time he took another 20s. from me for the oath I made, and [he did] *this unjustly.*" Can it be, considering these two latter entries, that the odious seizure of a deceased woman's cows was in some sense just? *Petrus de Bag* claimed that he had been forced to pay 12s. "because," in his words, "I married my daughter in Cerdanya and he made [me] redeem her." Or again: "I *Bernardus de Boxó* engaged my daughter to a husband and before the marriage took place she was killed by lightning, wherefore R. de Ribes took 28s. from me." Listen, on the other hand, to *Pere Amad,* from whom Raimund seized "one good cow, *for what reason I do not know.*" *Ermessen* and her husband were relieved of 5s. "because our young son died, *no other reason [causa].*" One more example: *Bernardus Duran* and his brother *Guilelmus* were forced between them to pay a total of 200s. "for many unjust occasions."[41]

From these accounts I must conclude that in the Ribes valley toward 1165–1175 some "causes" or "occasions" for demanding payments were considered "just."[42] If the peasants themselves ad-

---

40. *LFM,* ii, no. 580; *CC,* v, 73–75; *FAC,* i, 185.
41. R1-3433, R2-3217. My emphasis in preceding quotations.
42. For the judicial background of the "causes" see Bonnassie, *La Catalogne,* ii, 560–566, 580–584, 588–590.

mitted as much, it hardly seems necessary to ask Raimund de Ribes
what he thought. The "taking away" of money (beyond tenurial
payments, which are never mentioned) was always unwelcome,
the peasants thought, but not apparently always unjust. By ac-
knowledging that some seizures were "for cause" the peasants were
drawn, perhaps unwittingly, into recognizing a custom of exploitative lordship that is more advanced than anything yet tolerated in
the comital domains of the lowlands and the frontier. Raimund de
Ribes is not more brutal than his counterparts at Terrassa or Font-
rubí but his arbitrariness is more practiced—more customary. It
provokes a desperate *cri de coeur,* to be sure; and the threat to flee
may be a sign that afflictive lordship was still perceived by some to
be a wicked novelty. It was also a sign of suffering in common, as
elsewhere. Yet there is no evocation of a better past. The poign-
ancy attaches to individual lamentations. Raimund took away my
best cow, said *Guilelmus Petri,* "because I furtively received two
cheeses when I was hungry, so I was never afterward able to
work."[43] These are resigned as well as desperate people.

The Legitimation of Arbitrary Lordship

And so their voices fade out. Were they heeded?—or even heard at
all? Some in the localities must have thought it worth the trouble to
complain, for a diminishing stream of memorials flows into the
thirteenth century. But the results must have been discouraging.
No judicial response is visible in the records of courtiers who
certainly preserved some of the accounts of malfeasance addressed
to Raimund Berenguer IV and Alfons I, and who also preserved
judgments on other issues affecting the great families of the land.
The days were long past when the king's officials met peasants in
their courts and heard and judged their disputes over communal
interests. All I can say is that the memorials—at least, those that

43. R2-3217.

survive—commonly reached the Lord-Prince's companions. And that means that in his last years the great Lord-Count Raimund, who died in 1162, knew of these charges.

Which explains why there was surely some response to the charges. Whatever the procedures, it looks as if the Lord-King's protectorate of peasants was restored in most of his domains in the later twelfth century. At Caldes de Malavella and Llagostera Arnal de Perella failed to establish an exploitative lordship, although not for lack of trying. In 1183 his son Bernard lost his claim to certain houses, manses, and other entitlements at Caldes; his neighbors testified that the houses had been built for the King. But Bernard then retained much of his paternal inheritance, which suggests that Arnal had come to terms with his accusers. There were still no castles in these parishes adjoining the route to Occitania; King Alfons continued to commend agrarian tenures to village entrepreneurs in return for their supply of provisions.[44] At Terrassa, where the bailiwick remained independent of the castellany, we hear of no complaint after Deusde's time; while at Lower Corró there was some expansion of the King's direct lordship in the 1170s and 1180s.[45] Complaints from the old lowland domains from the Llobregat to the Tet faded out in the reign of Alfons I.

It is possible that franchisal communities of a traditional kind survived into the thirteenth century in some of these places. The people of Caldes de Malavella, Llagostera, Gavà, Terrassa, and Corró are not known to have received charters, so it may be worth noticing in this connection that their memorials of complaint include no charges against the Count or the King. If the bailiffs in these places were allies of the villagers, as seems to have been the case at Gavà and Caldes, and perhaps also at Terrats and elsewhere, privileges were not required. It is for places where the allegations did sometimes extend to the Lord-Prince or his bailiffs that we find

---

44. *LFM,* i, no. 400; ACA, Cancelleria, pergamins Alfons I, 359, 446, 447; *FAC,* i, 174, 176; ii, no. 101.

45. *FAC,* i, 169, 171.

evidence of charters and associative resistance. The people of Cabra agreed to pay 100 morabetins at Christmas "for commutation of tallage" in 1194, while those of Font-rubí rendered 100 quarters of grain yearly. When his bailiffs pestered the bishop's tenants at Font-rubí, Alfons bestowed a privilege on the church of Barcelona.[46]

But the successes of the Count's (and King's) tenants were severely qualified at best. They were hardly a defeat of arbitrary lordship. It was easier to dampen the ambitions of an upstart like Arnal de Perella than the plunderings of castellans like Pere de Bell-lloc or Berenguer de Clariana. For the franchisal communities were like clearings in a thickening jungle of seigneurial violence and exploitation. If Count Raimund Berenguer IV rewarded his faithful sworn barons, some of them doubtless his companions-in-arms, with fiefs on his old domains, could he realistically expect them to treat his peasants other than men of their class treated their own? The frontier, the expeditions against Muslims, and the conquests, to say nothing of association with mighty crusading warriors from across the Pyrenees, had whetted an insatiable appetite for wealth and status. We must try for once to see matters from their point of view. To a Berenguer de Bleda the lament that gouges on peasants were unprecedented may have seemed a laughable impertinence; what was new, surely, was the effort to curtail them. And that effort, such as it was, soon became threatening.

For it is altogether likely that prelates and advisers of Alfons I had the troubles in franchisal villages in mind when they undertook to impose a territorial Peace on Catalonia in 1173. Here the microhistory of power intersects with a major event of the later twelfth century: the institution of offices and obligations in the service of public order and security. Not for more than a century had there been so concerted an effort to superimpose government on the counties and multiplying lordships of the old Spanish March. It was

46. *CPC*, i[1], no. 200; Arxiu Capitular de Barcelona, "Libri antiquitatum" iv, fol. 119 (Joseph Mas, *Notes històriques del bisbat de Barcelona*, 12 vols. [Barcelona, 1906–1915], xii, no. 2201); *CSC*, iii, no. 1243.

an ambitious scheme, indeed an aggressive one, by which the Lord-King attempted not only to turn the vicars into accountable policemen of the Peace, with the power to constrain intransigent malefactors by force, but also to limit the militarism of magnates in their own domains; worse still, the magnates were required to swear to uphold the statutes that clipped their wings. It is no wonder that some resisted, forcing public confrontations with the Lord-King in great Corts at Girona (1188), Barcelona (1190?), and Barbastro (1192). And the conflict went badly for the kings and their clerical allies. Under Pere I (1196–1213) the barons tried to expand their exemptions from what they spoke of contemptuously as the "peace and truce of the lord king" (1202), and in this same Cort King Pere conceded "that if lords maltreat [*male tractaverint*] their peasants or take things away from them," they are not answerable to the Lord-King "in anything" unless they hold fiefs of the King or of churches.[47]

With this famous provision we come close to a theory of bad lordship. If the barons themselves could speak openly of their inflictions and seizures as abuses immune from external sanctions, then a whole category of seigneurial violence was vindicated against the aggressive tendencies of the Peace. Was this not virtually to legitimate practices against which the Lord-Princes' peasants had protested? Yet as we have seen those protests themselves were tainted with acquiescence. The peasants of Ribes who denounced seizures for intestacy or sterility were sure that these were wrong, not so sure they were unjust. At Caldes and Llagostera the payments for the vicar's quittance have a suspiciously routine appearance; exactions associated with alleged transgressions had become customary. Nor were the Count-Kings and their bailiffs disposed to resist the spread of lucrative customs that strengthened their control of rural manpower. By 1179 *intestia, exorchia,* and *cugucia*—respectively, payments on occasions of intestacy, death without heirs, and

47. T. N. Bisson, *Medieval France and her Pyrenean Neighbours: Studies in Early Institutional History* (London, 1989), pp. 140–151, 223–229; *CPT*, no. 21.

adultery—figured among the king's rightful (or rather, just?) revenues at Font-rubí and they are found soon afterward in the bailiwicks of Vilamajor, Sant Feliu de Llobregat, Terrassa, and Moià.[48]
What is more, the royal servants themselves were not loathe to
admit that such exactions were "bad usages" from which it required the royal grace to exempt. In his charter of 1163 the child-
King is made to say that he dispenses the men of Barcelona from
"all bad usages [mali usatici] imposed by his father's predecessors . . .
except for what I retain in exorchiae."[49] Here already the "bad customs" (Catalan: mals usos) of later notoriety make their appearance,
for exorchia (the fine on collateral inheritance, when not identical
with that on intestacy) was among the recognized burdens of what
came to be known as remença serfdom. And if the King himself can
lay claim to a "bad usage" as such, I have to suspect that he was of
no mind to launch a zealous assault on seigneurial prerogatives.
What he did oppose—or more likely his prelates, such as Bishop
Guillem de Torroja, who manifestly counselled that he reorganize
the old Peace and Truce to this end—was the more arbitrary and
brutal manifestations of protection (baiulia) as exercised by his own
men and of the depredations of warfare.

Remença servitude was to have a long history in Catalonia. Nothing like it survived in other west European lands. In a region
corresponding nearly (not exactly) to that represented in the memorials of complaint, peasants paid some or all of the "bad customs" to their lords, or paid heavily to be freed, for some 300 years.
The system came to seem scandalous to some by the early fifteenth
century, it was caught up in a civil war fought mainly over other
issues, and was abolished by royal decree in 1486.[50] The memorials

48. FAC, ii, nos. 34, 110, 111, 114, 116; cf. no. 124.
49. CPC, i[1], no. 120.
50. See chiefly Paul Freedman, Origins of Peasant Servitude in Catalonia, who
cites and moves beyond an extensive literature; also below, p. 132. For France, cf.
William C. Jordan, From Servitude to Freedom: Manumission in the Sénonais in the
Thirteenth Century (Philadelphia, 1986).

of complaint show that *remença* (redemption) had already an ominously customary meaning toward 1150–1160. Every seizure, every oath, every occasion—and almost every act of violence—could be redeemed, ransomed. That was the real problem in the Ribes valley, but it is evident everywhere else as well.[51] It is the same new insistence on jurisdictional power that appears also in northern France, only it is less restrained in Catalonia, less regulated and hardly less blatantly fiscal, than in France.[52] It is in this circumstance as well as in the clustering of customary exactions that our memorials of complaint point to an awareness of chronic disorder that marks the origin of the *remença* problem in Catalonia.

But redemption remained an ambiguous concept as well as a pervasive one in the twelfth century. In practice it might be an act of capricious violence, such as the seizure of *A. de Muntfred* until he "redeemed 300s.,"[53] but it might otherwise be a pacification. It was a purchase, and as in any market transaction the purchaser's satisfaction was not guaranteed. The townspeople of Vic who paid a "redemption of the coinage" to Pere I in 1197 were buying the Lord-King's promise to hold the coinage stable, to forego an arbitrary mutation; yet it is clear from an abortive project to limit the Lord-King's prerogatives in 1205 that for some Catalans ransoms of coinage were no less arbitrary than novel exactions of other sorts, including debasements of coinage.[54] On the other hand, the men at Cabra who commuted the King's arbitrary *questia* into a fixed annual payment toward 1194 were purchasing a release from violence

---

51. R1-3433, R2-3217. At Cabra (Ca1-2609) the bailiff Bertran de Vilafranca had collected a tax *(missio)* for the King toward 1175, and "when it was all paid Bertran took away from *Petrus de Albi* his donkey and they redeemed it for 3s." See also *FAC*, ii, no. 124 (discussed below at n. 59).

52. Georges Duby, *The Early Growth of the European Economy: Warriors and Peasants from the Seventh to the Twelfth Century*, tr. Howard B. Clarke (London, 1974), pp. 227–229.

53. Ca1-2609.

54. T. N. Bisson, *Conservation of Coinage: Monetary Exploitation and its Restraint in France, Catalonia, and Aragon (c. A.D. 1000–c. 1225)* (Oxford, 1979), pp. 83–91.

that surely improved their lot.[55] It is worth noting, however, that the King reserved his justice (*placita*) at Cabra while making no (explicit) mention of *intestia, exorchia,* and *cugucia.* Could it be that these were implicitly reserved in exchange for the renunciation of unexcused taxation?

Some such exchange must at any rate have occurred in lowland domains of the old county of Barcelona. Few of these places received charters of privilege. Their old franchisal status persisted as the count-kings continued to exploit them directly, or to commend them temporarily. For these domains the fiscal accounts surviving in a series beginning in the 1170s show that the Lord-King routinely collected what were now called the "five" (or "six) causes"—that is, arson (*arsina*), *cugucia, exorchia, intestaciones,* homicide (*homicidia*), and sometimes wreck (*troba*)—but not tallage or *questia.*[56] Where *questiae* do figure (in these domains), as at Barcelona and Caldes de Malavella, they have the appearance of regulated impositions.[57] Out of the stress and distress described by the peasants, it seems, had come a bargain by which capricious bullying and violence were exchanged for contingent fines. In the domains of abiding value to the Count-Kings a direct and reformed management had done the work for which charters were required elsewhere.

Yet it was a tainted compromise at best. It sanctioned a custom of tenurial exactions (however regulated) whose legitimacy was held in doubt by the Count-Kings and barons alike (to say nothing of peasants). Nor was the compromise speedily effected in upland domains. In Cerdanya and the Berguedà the counts of Barcelona had inherited the new mode of afflictive lordship, from which they

55. *CPC,* i[1], no. 200.
56. *FAC,* ii, nos. 34, 110, 111, 114, 116, 118, 124.
57. *CPC,* i[1], no. 120; *FAC,* ii, nos. 101, 125. It is clear that while the despised exactions were sometimes clustered (citations in n. 56), the cluster varies and is not yet identified as such with servile status. See, however, *FAC,* ii, no. 124, discussed below at n. 59.

seldom dispensed.[58] At Moià as late as 1209 King Pere I pledged the
honor to his creditor Berenguer de Riera with the whole array of
revenues, including "quests," "tolts," "forces," "ransoms of people," *cuguciae, exorchiae, intestiae,* "and everything belonging to us in
whatsoever manner, just or unjust."[59] It would be difficult to imagine a better invitation—or a more legitimate one—to exercise an
arbitrary lordship.

★   ★   ★

These consequences may seem far removed from the troubled
villagers voiced in the memorials. But I hear some resonance of
their petitions in an enlarged history of power of which the human
stakes and intonations are lost in the normative laconic records of
constitutional struggle. And there could well have been perplexity
as the memorials came in. It was a real issue how far King Alfons
himself and the handful of prelates and barons committed to his
interest could subject themselves to the beneficent lordship over
peasants and churches they tried to impose on the the baronage.
For the King, like his great father, must, deep down, have shared
the lordly outlook of the elite families. Is it not likely that in his
eagerness to mobilize credit and service in the giddy days of his
grand conquests, Raimund Berenguer IV not only commended
vicariates as if they were fiefs in his old domains but even encour-
aged his "faithful men" to exploit them freely? Whatever the circumstances and terms of these commissions to men like Deusde
and Berenguer de Bleda, it would appear that the Lord-Count

58. *FAC,* ii, nos. 1MNOP, 8, 10,E, 11, 17, 19, 46, 53, 76, 112B, etc. One may
plot geographically the incidence of indexed citations to *questia (chestia)* to show
that Manresa (no. 32) and Moià (no. 124; cf., however, no. 116: no mention of
questia) lay just outside the new franchisal zone. Royal domains in Berguedà,
Cerdanya (and Ribes), and Roussillon remained burdened with "bad customs"
(*mals usos*), save for chartered exemptions, as at Puigcerdà and Collioure (*CPC,* i[1],
nos. 166, 223); these exemptions are more inclusive than those in the old comital
lowland domains.

59. *FAC,* ii, no. 124. This is already a *remença* lordship.

regarded their recipients as allies rather than as administrators. Their support and fidelity defined such public order as existed. They swore to keep faith to their lord, nothing more, viewing their commissions not as the condition of service but as reward. This was a feudal outlook, precisely speaking, for it was the tenement, often called "fief" (*fevum*),[60] that defined the relationship; and it is clear that the proprietary sense of the fief encroaches on the administrative. Men of such outlook took easily to the harsh modes of lordship so widely practised by the castral aristocracy.

The commissions of justice and the protectorate created virtual lordships in the comital domains, not agencies. That is what the unreformed vicariates were, and I cannot see that Raimund Berenguer IV himself expected otherwise. It was left to the villagers and bailiffs to protest and in so doing to counterpose the image of an old order in which the lord-counts' benign protectorate had fostered freedoms and moral cohesion that were now being threatened or destroyed. This image was tendentious but not false. Its projection reveals the sturdy survival of the concept of fiscal administration at the level of the bailiwick. For *their* fiefs or portions bailiffs were expected to serve the Count instead of themselves and to observe the *capbreus*. No doubt the reality was often different, for "bailiwick" (*baiulia*) had come to be regarded customarily as an exploitation as well as an agency.[61] Bertran de Vilafranca, assuming some truth in the charges against him, cannot have been the only heavy-handed bailiff; while at Caldes de Malavella and Llagostera, where the old bailiffs seem to have identified with the people to denounce the corruption of their function, it may be that their own ambitions were thwarted by vicarial distraints. Yet for all this the memory of a serene comital protectorate was a sincere and plausible representation of villagers and bailiffs toward 1150; and the Count-Prince's courtiers and judges, whatever their own con-

---

60. Ibid., i, no. 1.
61. *Glossarium mediae latinitatis Cataloniae*, cols. 216–220 (s.v. *baiulia*).

fusions about lordship, must have been receptive. For the memorials were a timely reminder that the transcendant dimension of comital power, such as was celebrated in the *Usatges,* was threatened by the unchecked diffusion of exploitative customary lordship.

Yet the response took some time. The Lord-Princes had time because the rural protests were uncoordinated, pointing to no worse resistance than threats to abandon tenements in the vehemently eloquent pleas for remedy. So the crisis which ensued was not so much that of the "franchises" as of a newly abrasive confrontation between the barons and castellans and King Alfons and his adherents in the 1180s. And in this conflict we can see from the statutes that the treatment of peasants and churches in or bordering on the baronial domains took priority over circumstances in the Lord-King's domains and protectorates. For the latter the institution of a newly attentive written accountability together with the disciplining and replacement of vicars and bailiffs was a sufficient response to the memorials of complaint. But nothing had been done to discipline the lordship and bellicosity of barons who, like Viscount Arnal de Castellbò in the 1180s, persisted in the violent customs deplored in the memorials and prohibited by the statutes. And in their bitter obstinacy can be glimpsed that subsistent taste for violence which produced widening waves of trouble for the peasants, churches, and rulers of Catalonia.[62]

The lords in this little world were warriors, armed with weapons that were their playthings from childhood, mounted so as to look down on people as well as to escape danger. Their habits of coercion, distraint, and physical or afflictive violence were surely nurtured in their bellicosity. Accordingly, I do not wish to distinguish very sharply between the violences of war and of lordship. As Josep Maria Salrach has well shown, the prevailing types of violence

---

62. *CPT,* nos. 14–18; *FAC,* i, ch. 3; T. N. Bisson, "The War of the Two Arnaus: A Memorial of the Broken Peace in Cerdanya (1188)," *Miscel.lània en homenatge al P. Agustí Altisent* (Tarragona, 1991), pp. 95–107.

changed from the tenth to the twelfth centuries, with the stress on pillage becoming ever more characteristic.[63] Our peasants of the memorials knew pillage when they suffered from it, as at Gavà, Corró, and Argençola; they were pretty good at distinguishing between oppressions petty, greedy, and brutal; but they seldom help me tell a lord apart from a warrior. This is surprising, in a way, for it is hard to understand why any lord would have wished to oppress his own tenants. And indeed it appears that for all the troubles reported at Caldes de Malavella, Ribes, and Cabra, the violence told of their masters was less brutal than elsewhere, more nearly tolerable. Yet the image of plunder haunts even the descriptions of routines of power, as in accounts of impositions at Font-rubí, Cabra, and Castellvell, where tallage seems little more than apportioned and heralded pillage, to say nothing of the itemized seizures at Terrassa, Ribes, and Argençola. It is hard to avoid the conclusion that economic warfare created the habits and techniques we see in allegations of afflictive coercion and constraint. And it is not hard to understand why in the renewal of the Peace and Truce that began in 1173 the clergy prevailed on the young Lord-King to extend the protections he would help secure to the "safe places" associated with churches and cemeteries, thus at a stroke expanding the spaces within which persons regardless of their allegiances could hope for shelter from seizures and afflictive violence. Our villagers knew about such hopes and expectations. *Arnallus Raimundi* suffered a seizure in church on an Easter Sunday at Font-rubí, *Guilelmus Iohanis* was dragged from church at Corró and imprisoned, while at Cabra, Bertran de Vilafranca, having failed to seize a bailiff "by force," did better by luring him to sanctuary (*salvitas*), where he held and ransomed him for 100s.[64] Yet violations of sanctuary were seldom charged in the memorials,

63. Salrach, "Agressions senyorials," pp. 11–29.
64. F1–3409, Co3214, Ca2–3474.

which doubtless only means that most outrages took place elsewhere.[65]

Force and violence were means of power even in those places—the ones whose people complained—where the authority of the Lord-Princes might have been expected to limit them. They cannot have been less blatant or shocking in the baronial domains, where most peasants lived. Everywhere habits of violence and constraint were becoming customary because they were associated with claims to social superiority. The Lord-Princes were in no position to repudiate such claims, having long since traded the protectorate of their peasants for a productive solidarity with the castral nobility. A new class longer on ambition than on resources was in the making, a class for which a mode of bad lordship cynically acknowledged was jeopardized by the complaints at a moment when it seemed to have attained the sanctity of territorial custom. Peasants were the treasure of Catalonia. Should they be plundered or administered? The issue was less simple for the Count-Kings than for the castled barons and knights—and to that extent the peasants of the old Catalan counties were the losers.

65. See the masterly article by Pierre Bonnassie, "Les *sagreres* catalanes: la concentration de l'habitat dans le "cercle de paix" des églises," in *L'environnement des églises et la topographie religieuse des campagnes médiévales,* ed. M. Fixot and E. Zadora-Rio (Paris, 1994), pp. 68–79.

[IV]

CULTURE

Some of these people are known to us by name, their voices reverberating in their written grievances. Can I not hear *Oliba* at Terrats, who said he owed the Count maintenance for three knights and three squires and two sextars of feedgrain? Or *R. Rodlan* at Valmala, who said he had a parcel of land at *Sorial* free of obligation? Or the widow *Gitarda* at Pardines, who said that Raimund de Ribes took away eighteen sheep "unjustly"? Or *Martinus* at Font-rubí, who related the pathetic story of being dispossessed, he and his family, of his own houses and rooms so that he "sustained great disgrace and shame"? Their voices, I say; but were these *their* words? Was it not in reality someone else who conveyed these assertions and stories?[1]

Indeed, there *were* others who first rapped at doors, who convoked the people or extracted this information. I have mentioned them often: the scribes, the bailiffs, the obscurely reticent sympathizers perhaps sometimes two deep in my ranks of informants, and almost all of them anonymous. Only at Esclet and Ganix does *Guilelmus Ponci* seem to give himself away, and even there only in the words of a scribe himself nameless. At Cabra Bertran de Vila-

1. Tts3283, V3202, R1-3433, F2-3141.

franca speaks (and writes?) in authentic accents, but as a rival of his peasants' tormentors.[2] Yet not even the mediated narrations quite drown out the clamor of indignation and passion sounding in words evidently once spoken as well as written. Or so I persist in believing.

Is this a delusion of mine? The experts teach us that "popular culture" is, in Peter Burke's words, "an elusive quarry." Even if one accepts some appropriately modified form of Robert Redfield's distinction between "great" and "little traditions," it does not simply follow that we can discern specifically and peculiarly popular modes of behavior through the literate representations of those who seem different from the people they record. But the difficulty of interpreting the attitudes of the peasants who inhabit our memorials lies not so much in the distortions of transmitted evidence as in the overlapping identity of the human groups in question. Here it was not a matter of interrogations into suspicious beliefs, as with the shepherds of Montaillou or the miller of Friuli. Far from misrepresenting the grievances they heard, the Catalan inquirers and scribes virtually identified with them. The warmly subjective forms of expression from Font-rubí, Corró, the Ribes valley, and Argençola, when considered with the moralizing of complaint almost everywhere in the comital domains, point to a characteristic solidarity of sympathetic comprehension. Sympathy need not guarantee the fidelity of representation, it is true, but there is a further consideration in this case. The men who carried out the inquiries first envisaged by Count Raimund Berenguer IV cannot have seemed unfamiliar to their subjects. If the anonymous courtiers who mobilized the peasants and scribes included men of knightly rank, such as Bertran de Castellet, they were already habituated to an anti-knightly policy. As for the scribes, surely men well known in their localities, their literacy cannot have been such as to deform the transmission, nor does their variable latinity sug-

2. Ca1-2609.

gest the slightest difficulty of comprehension. Everywhere the spoken vernacular easily made up for failures of the written language, a
vernacular the scribes spoke as well as their subjects. I do not mean
to minimize our own difficulties with these memorials of complaint. But the people who produced them were hardly mandarins
imposing alien perspectives.[3]

What seems more problematic is how far the rural societies
represented in the memorials of complaint formed a population
with common cultural characteristics. Consider the matters of language and habitats. I have no hesitation in believing that *Raimundus
Gunter* at Terrats could have conversed easily with *Bernardus Eneg* at
Caldes de Malavella or with *Raimundus Marti* at Font-rubí or with
Arnaldus de Ual irana at Cabra. The spoken vernacular of all the
Lord-Princes' peasants and tenants was already manifestly that form
of Catalan well known to philologists as "preliterary Catalan." Although every memorial was composed in Latin, every single one
contains vernacular forms of striking diversity: appellatives (like
batle=bailiff, Appendix 4, no. 1), dispositions (*merced*=mercy, 6;
paor=fear, 14), clothing and furnishings (*camises*=shirts, 16;
touaies=cloths or towels, 16), and proper names and toponyms (*Bernardus Eneg,* 4; *Guiem Sinfre,* 9; *ad Cigár,* 2; *Pegeres,* 9), to say
nothing of simple deformations from Latin (*adúc*=*adhuc,* until now,
12). In respect to their common tongue the peasants of the comital
domains were but a subset of that larger rural population evoked in
Chapter II; nor can I see that their visitors and scribes were any
different, either in their familiar speech—which we know through
them—or in their latinity.[4]

3. See generally Peter Burke, *Popular Culture in Early Modern Europe* (New
York, 1978; rev., 1994); the quoted words are the title of his ch. 3. Also Robert
Redfield, *Peasant Society and Culture: An Anthropological Approach to Civilization*
(Chicago, 1956); Le Roy Ladurie, *Montaillou;* and Carlo Ginzburg, *The Cheese and
the Worms: The Cosmos of a Sixteenth-Century Miller,* tr. John and Anne Tedeschi
(London, 1980 [1976]).

4. See generally Antoni M. Badia i Margarit, *La formació de la llengua catalana.
Assaig d'interpretació histórica.* Publicacions de l'Abadia de Montserrat (Badalona,

Yet as appeared in Chapter II, the people whose voices we hear formed dispersed and distinct societies. Only by rare accident could *Maienca* of Llagostera ever have encountered the widow *Gitarda* of Pardines, let alone anyone from Font-rubí or Argençola. Of their villages only Corró, Terrassa, and Gavà were within a day's ride of each other; most were much farther distant. Moreover, they occupied diverse habitats: the villagers of Caldes de Malavella and Llagostera adjoining the great comital highway to which they were suppliers of grain, wine, and maintenance; those of the Ribes valley oriented toward a household economy of sheepherding and upland pursuits; and both societies distinctive in their customs of traditional settlement. The peoples of Barcelona's hinterlands were likewise of generations-long descent, but theirs was a history disrupted by Almoravid campaigns within living memory, their economies oriented toward the recent prosperity of Barcelona. Font-rubí, Cabra, and Argençola were the diverse and less firmly settled outposts of serrated horizons in lands ceasing to be frontiers without ceasing to be violent; places where castellans replaced the Moors in popular fears. Considered in their ecologies, economies, and customs of property, these were microsocieties within the undifferentiated masses descended from the mountaineers of the ancient Spanish March. And it is possible that one or more of the tenets and beliefs revealed in the memorials of complaint was peculiar to its place.

Revealed, I say: it was a matter of revelation. Except in one important respect what is recounted in the memorials about customs, values, and beliefs is disclosed incidentally; made known not because people were asked about it but because it was entailed in their responses. A good example is found in the complaints from the Ribes valley, where the people who lamented exactions when

---

1982); Joan Bastardas, *La llengua catalana mil anys enrere*. Biblioteca de Cultura Catalana 79 (Barcelona, 1995). For the purpose of this paragraph, I cite the records as numbered in Appendix 4.

their siblings died—*Guilelm Alinád, Felix* "the peasant"—witnessed inadvertently to the implantation of a servile imposition on occasion of intestacy.[5] This means that the scope of cultural representation is limited, the very essence of inquisition registers is missing. I shall welcome the compensating sympathy of the writers in its place. Yet what is revealed cannot be much less than all we can know about this rural culture.

Customary Solidarities

"And on account of this loss he separated himself thence, he and his family, and we don't know where he lives . and along with him we lost three other companions who are in another land . and now we don't know where they are nor just what they lost . but we know for sure that they lost all they possessed." This is how the people of Argençola remembered *Berengarius Maria*. They remembered that he had been one of them, he and his household, while making admirably clear that *his* loss of property was matched by *their* loss of him and his. And they regretted "three other companions" who had gone they knew not where. Their recollection dwelt on companionship and its destruction, while evoking also the solidarity of family. And I think it likely that the scribe conveyed yet a third sense of association by the expression *separauit se inde* ("he separated himself thence"), words seeming to evoke a commmunity of Argençola extending beyond the "companionship."

Of these rural solidarities the "family" was fundamental. Nurturing the affections of trust and support, it was the remedy of impotent life. The *familia* so often mentioned in the memorials was the household of parents and children, perhaps often with grandparents, such as fled from Argençola with *Berengarius Maria*. The disrupted family of *Martinus* at Font-rubí was surely an extended one,

5. R1-3433.

given the amplitude of its lodgings. Yet even such peasant families as these must have included persons beyond the circle of blood-relatives, as was certainly the case of Arnal de Perella's *familia* at Caldes and Llagostera and Berenguer de Bleda's at Font-rubí. The slaves ("Saracens as well as Christians") and animals of Berenguer's household and the "friends, elders, and kinsfolk" of Arnal's were emblematic of their pretensions to great lordship. And there is an arresting congruence in the ways these solidarities were described as living organisms: Berenguer de Bleda was said to "collect *albergas* with his family and squander [them] in his houses," while the memorialist of Caldes de Malavella stresses the presumptuous con-bibularity of Arnal de Perella and his entourage, adding that only the appearance of the Lord-Count's family could interrupt it.[6] The quasi-lordly *familia* of rural Catalonia seems to project a sympto-matic Mediterranean sociability, one as much envied as deplored by the peasants. Their own families were commonly evoked less in their affective expressivity than in their disrupted domestic prosper-ity: the exodus of so many "young men" from thriving households at Caldes and Llagostera, the disappearance of *Berengarius Maria* and others from Argençola, the threats of flight, scarcely less eloquent, at Font-rubí and Cabra. Familial solidarity was rooted in the wealth of the *domus* as well as in affinities natural and useful; in the grain, wine, and money lost at Gavà, Terrassa, Ribes and almost every-where else; in the houses violated and persons afflicted at Terrassa, Font-rubí, and Argençola.

If the family partakes rather of culture than of power, the reverse may be true of community. The hint of associative loss at the end of the grievances from Argençola does not stand alone, it is true; the memorials from Corró and Font-rubí seem to spring from collective representations for which the scribes had no adequate formulary. Yet even in those places the writers implicitly treated

6. F2-3141, C-Ll-2501.

their subjects as tenants in personal dependence on the Lord-Count or his successor. The people were multiple, hence the need for the term "people" (*homines*), which figures in the protocols for Terrassa, Font-rubí, Cabra, and Argençola; yet nowhere does it yet imply political identity. Here, I suspect, the conceptual vocabulary lagged behind social and cultural realities. The notions of separation at Argençola and of exodus at Caldes and Llagostera, to say nothing of the undiluted collective lamentations at Font-rubí, point already to affective bondings arising from collective experience in old settlements.

More tenaciously insistent were the habits of fidelity, which fell on a continuum of values somewhere between family and community. Almost everywhere the peasants identified the lordship—that is, the knights—as well as the bad lord responsible for violence. At Gavà, Sant Climent, and Viladecans, where Guilelm de Sant Martí "broke into the village," *Bernardus Mironis* lost 10 quarters of barley when he tried to resist Guilelm's "men." The vicarial lords "and their men" inflicted the evils reported at Font-rubí; Berenguer de Clariana "with his horsemen" at Cabra, and (with) "his men" at Argençola; "for fear of those horsemen the people of Cabra dare not appeal to you [the Lord-King]."[7] Very surely the peasants (and scribes) appreciated the threatening dynamics of such knightly solidarities, so different from the Count's benign protectorate; indeed, if we are well informed about the situation at Caldes de Malavella and Llagostera, Arnal de Perella co-opted the Lord-Count's tenants into an abrasive band sworn to himself. Arnal's lordship, so far from being an alien phenomenon, was a natural sprout in its society. It took a uniquely scandalized scribe to represent it as a tumorous growth, although it is true that these villages are the only places where we hear of a coercive solidarity other than that of raiding knights.

7. Ca1-2609, F1–3 (3409, 3141, 3288), A3145.

Customary Moralities: Faith

Fidelity was a problematic value, for its moral implications were equivocal. The Lord-Princes' peasants implored the fidelity of protection, deplored that of exploitation. But as a rule they were represented as afflicted by violence, not by fidelity or its betrayal. They overlooked the psychic-associative springs of the violence from which they suffered, perhaps not unmindful that service owed its social merit (if any) to a lord's intentions. Berenguer de Clariana and Guilelm de Sant Martí did wrong to seize and expel, but no stricture was passed on the knights who profited by serving them faithfully. Only at Caldes de Malavella and Llagostera was an alleged violator stigmatized as disloyal to the Lord-Count, a representation that looks to our eyes like the most efficacious sort of appeal to such a ruler's interest.

And it was a characteristic assertion. For it was also at Caldes, and again only there, that an intermediary ventured an indignant account of oaths made and broken. Here is what he said:

> He [Arnal de Perella] made an oath for himself to certain men of Caldes that he would be their faithful [man] in everything. which he never observed to them . and some of them made an oath to him that [? they would be his] faithful men and because he did not keep his oath to them . they broke their oath to him. After these oaths were made and disregarded . never did the land do other than get worse . . . in bad storms . and there is no longer even half the people who lived in that village when their troubles came upon them.

Whatever its other causes, demoralization followed here from the violation of oaths of fidelity. Perhaps the writer meant also to suggest that the very swearing of such oaths was wrong, for in these villages as in the others the peasants' primary obligation was to their Lord-Prince. Yet entering into sworn compacts must have seemed a tempting means to profit in other villages as well. I think it safe to suppose that the solemnity of oaths was a tenet of rural culture in Catalonia.

This point matters because it is hard otherwise to discern specifically religious values in the memorials of complaint. Something of the Christian texture of most people's experience comes through, next to nothing of their baptismal or penitential beliefs. The people of Font-rubí beseeched Raimund Berenguer IV to renounce bad customs "through God and through His Mother" while those of Argençola were represented as appealing "to God and the King." Priests and monks were all about them—*Poncius* the clerk and *Raimundus* the monk at Caldes de Malavella, *Giu* the clerk at Font-rubí, the monks of Santes Creus around Cabra. The churches of Santa Maria and Sant Esteve at Caldes suffered infringement of their tithes. And there are signs, some of them already mentioned, that the times and spaces of Christian belief were associated with desires for peace and refuge. Seizures in churches were deplored at Font-rubí and Corró; a violation of sanctuary was reported at Cabra, while at Pardines the peasant *Iohanes Oliba* alleged that Raimund de Ribes "struck him at the church door." A notably brutal violation of the "truce of God" was charged against Berenguer de Castellvell.[8]

No doubt the people of these villages yearned for peace. They were used to the traditional devices of sanctuary associated with church buildings, cemeteries, and the asylum of thirty paces.[9] But there is little or no notice of this institution in the memorials, which have to do, in every case but that of Castellvell, with places in the direct domain and protectorate of the counts of Barcelona. Moreover, the reinstitution of the territorial Peace and Truce in 1173 and after, while it seems to have answered officially to the grievances, was a promotion of the greater clergy and barons then in control of the boy-King. It was justified in the Old-Testament

8. F1-3409 (face and dorse), A3145, C-Ll-2501, Ca2-3474, R1-3433, Cast3509.

9. Bonnassie, "Les *sagreres* catalanes."

ideology of upright kingship; peasants may have heard of this Peace
from the pulpit and, if so, have been comforted by it; but as it first
appeared in royal lands it was not so much a moral as a quasi-politi-
cal program directed against the barons and knights.[10] What was
exhorted of villagers was more likely the penitential doctrine of
Saint Paul, if the twelfth-century homilies discovered in the upland
parish of Organyà (county of Urgell) may be accepted as indicative.
And this doctrine, while bracing of character, may have been less
comforting.

The homilist of Organyà (possibly of Provençal identity) taught
love above all, and resignation. "Lords," he wrote, "charity is absti-
nence from evil" (*caritad és abstinència de mal*). "He who has charity
does not return evil for evil, and reconciles those who do evil."
Perhaps this Pauline morality held a touch of hope for due process
of petition: the charitable man "seeks right [*dretura*] and truth." But
the sermon continues: "That man, lords, who fears the world's
persecution, know that he has not perfect charity, for he who has
charity has no fear except of God." When "Our Lord" resisted the
Devil's tempting, "so he gave us an example that we should suffer
our enemies and shows that we should not render evil for evil, that
first we should have patience and humility," remembering that the
one tempted by the Devil "is the head of all people."[11]

Such exhortations might have been as consoling to the bad lords
of the villages as to their victims. Could it be that those peasants
induced to justify the demands or seizures they (otherwise) deplored were influenced by this penitential culture? Had they not
heard such preaching in their churches? There is no way to know
for sure. Yet I think it altogether likely that the manuscript of
Organyà preserves faithfully the very homiletics of charitable patience in an adverse world that was voiced in rural romanesque
churches—many still standing today, including some in the places

10. *CPT*, arengas to nos. 14, 15, on the office of the *rectus princeps*, recalling
Prov. 8.15: "Per me reges regnant et potentes scribunt iusticiam."

11. *Homilies d'Organyà*, ed. Coromines, pp. 48–50, 67.

that matter here—from the Ebro valley to the Rhône. In their Christian morality as in the names they bore, the people who pleaded for redress were like all the others in a far-flung Mediterranean rural culture. They knew about knights, knew about castles. They would have understood a preacher who expounded 1 Peter 3-11 (the Apostle here echoing Ps. 33.15): "Turn from evil and do good, seek after peace and follow it." And it was a hard lesson: "that man seeks peace and follows it who does no evil or injury to those who do him harm, for the love of Our Lord."[12]

Yet the peasants surely hoped to be forgiven for imperfect charity. It was for the transgressors to answer for misdeeds. They must have heard the sermons, too; but they could only have hoped to be justified on grounds of right or custom, hardly on those of conscience. Theirs was a rationale of social superiority by no means easy to resist. People like *Berengarius Bonifilii* and *Guilelm Alinád* in the Ribes valley seem to have thought that sterility or intestacy afforded excuse for the exactions they suffered. The memorials tell of worldly justice and its failure. Yet the penitential culture of peace may have had some influence in the restructuring of power in the later twelfth century. The statutes for the county of Urgell not only invoke the "divine majesty through which kings reign and the powerful uphold justice" (a reminiscence of Prov. 8.15–16, which had figured also in the King's statutes of 1173); they also quote from the Beatitudes on "peacemakers, blessed, for they shall be called sons of God" (Matt. 5.9); from Saint John (14.27; 20.21): "I leave you peace, my peace I give you" and "Peace be with you"; and from Saint Paul (1 Thess. 5.15). "Seek ye peace for each other and for all men," where the word "peace" has been substituted for "good." What is more, the apostolic words "to follow (seek after) peace" seem to have been drawn from homiletic discourse to assume a place in common parlance. The earliest allusions to reme-

---

12. Ibid., pp. 47–48. The church of Sant Jaume of Queralbs survives with its twelfth-century capitals, one of which depicts women and warriors, another the terrifying toothy heads of monsters (*CR*, x, 184–185).

dial armies of enforcement contain the expressions "to follow the peace and compel those who infringe it" (Béziers, 1170), "to follow the army" (of peace; Girona, 1188), and "to follow the peace in arms" (Montpellier, 1215). For the children of our villagers the enforcement of peace became an obligation hardly easier to bear than the forgiveness in which it was rooted.[13]

Customary Moralities: Honor and Shame

When *Arnaldus Garriga, Raimundus Gunter,* and their fellows at Terrats laid down the limits to the Count's maintenance, declaring that "he has no other rent whatsoever," they defined their right at once legally and morally. It would be wrong, their parchment proclaims, to demand more of them because that would be a violation of custom. This double-edged morality pervades the memorials of complaint. Sometimes it is explicit, as at Font-rubí, where the "people" deplored novel exactions which the Lord-Count had imposed on them and declared "that a great evil is written in this charter," and at Queralbs, where the "people" were said to be afflicted by "these evils and many others." Elsewhere it was implicit that seizures and demands were wrong, although some people, like *Petrus de Bag* and *Bernardus de Boxó* in the Ribes valley, seem to have thought the injuries they suffered might be justified. Everywhere the memorials give expression to indignation.

That is, the people were aroused in diverse ways to feel their distress emotionally, viscerally, as well as conscientiously. In fact, the cost to self-esteem must have been their deeper sense of affliction. The violation of God's peace cannot have troubled the victims as much as it did God, nor have induced many to grieve for the souls of their tormentors. But to be struck physically, as was *Guilelmus Gerouart*'s mother at Terrassa and *Iohanes Macíp* at Quer-

---

13. *CPT,* nos. 16, 17 (c. 14); *HL,* viii, 275–276; *Sacrorum conciliorum nova et amplissima collectio,* ed. J. Mansi, 31 vols. (Florence, 1759–98), xxii, 948, c. 39.

albs and so many others everywhere, was to suffer the very indig-
nity that aroused indignation. It was to have one's inferiority
confirmed, enforced. When a kinsman of *Petrus Rastan* of Ribes
suffered blows of spurs at the hands (or feet?) of Raimund de Ribes,
leaving him bedridden until death, was he not being ridden like an
ill-fed nag?

The culture of honor and shame, like so much else in their
experience, is largely concealed in memorials whose writers took
for granted a prevailing social gulf between the villagers and their
tormentors. I do not mean that all injuries were felt to shame or
demean. When Bertran de Vilafranca allegedly threw *Alegretus Ferrarius* out of Cabra "on account of many wrongs which he did to
him," this looks like an incident of petty feud.[14] Many other allegations are devoid of the sort of personal or circumstantial detail that
would allow inferences about the emotional facets of resentment.
Yet there is reason to believe that in societies where the superiority
of knights, vicars, and bailiffs was by no means so assured as such
men could have wished, the people who charged them were anx-
ious about their status, about the ulterior meaning of the pressures
they deplored. Not all of this would get through the formality of
attestation. As Julian Pitt-Rivers observes, "An inferior is not
deemed to possess sufficient honour to resent the affront of a supe-
rior."[15] Yet some of the afflicted peasants surely did feel dishonored
in their injuries, for they said so categorically.

Listen again to *Martinus de Fonterubeo,* whose complaint forms
the most extended illustration of shaming to be found in the memorials:

14. Ca2-3474.

15. Julian Pitt-Rivers, *The Fate of Shechem, or the Politics of Sex: Essays in the
Anthropology of the Mediterranean* (Cambridge, 1977), p. 10. See also *Honor and
Shame and the Unity of the Mediterranean,* ed. David D. Gilmore. Publications of the
American Anthropological Association 22 (Washington, 1987), especially (Gil-
more), "Introduction: The Shame of Dishonor" (pp. 2–21) and Stanley Brandes,
"Reflections on Honor and Shame in the Mediterranean," pp. 121–134, who
points to a useful disentangling of the concepts of honor and shame.

B. de Bleda came with all his *familia*, Saracens as well as Christians, dogs as well as animals, into his house, and he did this with great force and against *Martinus'* will and he built a stone oven there . and stayed there with all his *familia* five weeks . and resided in his upper houses . and *Martinus* lived below with his family . and there *Martinus* suffered great shame and great disgrace in his houses . and when B. de Bleda went away from the aforesaid place he took 11s. from *Martinus*. Another time B. de Bleda took 20s. from the said *Martinus* because of a certain honor he agreed to give him which he did not give him [i.e., Berenguer to *Martinus*] . nor had he [Berenguer] the right to bestow that honor . and another time B. de Bleda lodged with the aforesaid *Martinus* willfully with all his *familia* and [?publicly] made *Martinus* confirm his right and he [took from] him 2 quarters of wheat . and made him carry those 2 quarters of wheat to his donkey at Bleda by great force.[16]

Martinus of Font-rubí felt violated in his house, his household. That above all. He and his were put down, literally: *deorsum* is the Latin word; not merely inconvenienced but also ejected from their preferred rooms, "greatly shamed in their [own] houses." For it was social presumption for Berenguer and his entourage to commandeer the buildings of these prosperous people of Font-rubí, who were forced into lesser as well as lower space; who, unable to welcome those who had evicted them, could only suffer their disdain; who, quite simply, were made to feel like servants. They became, I conjecture, like their poorer neighbors, losing face with them as well as amongst themselves—for their own *familia*, after all; their own honor, indeed—rested on service. What had happened was outrageous, a "great shame and great disgrace."

The more nearly routine allegations which follow should be understood in this light. *Martinus* had been offended personally as well as domestically; he wanted the scribe to record two seizures of money, a further arbitrary requisition of lodging with *Martinus*, the

16. F2-3141.

latter's forced recognition of Berenguer's (lordly) right (*directum*), and what looks like a demeaning demand that *Martinus* himself carry sacks of grain taken from him against his will. One of the seizures of money was pegged to the promise of an unspecified honor which *Martinus* claimed never was fulfilled, adding that Berenguer lacked the "power" to dispose of this honor. In its context, this murky detail points to personal resentment of Berenguer's presumption, as does, more certainly, the charge that Berenguer made *Martinus* carry the grain to his tormentor's donkey. *Martinus* felt violated in his honor, his estate (not his manliness), and felt the shame of humiliation.

Housebreakings and evictions were reported elsewhere. Guilelm de Sant Martí's bailiff forced *Bertrandus'* house at Sant Climent and stole a pig. The violation of *Carbo*'s house at Font-rubí was linked to the prosecution of a debt; while at Cabra, *G. de Concabella* alleged that Bertran de Vilafranca's bailiff had broken into his house together "with men of Montblanc."[17] None of these violations was described as shameful, merely as iniquitous. There was a difference between requisitioning for tenancy and seizures or impositions by way of hospitality, such as were defined by limitation at Terrats but were alleged as wrongful violence at Gavà and Font-rubí, and may have been concealed in the itemized claims of seizures at Terrassa, Llagostera, Valmala, Cabra, and indeed almost everywhere. But in one respect all such violence replicated the plight of *Martinus de Fonterubeo*: it represented force as confirming inferiority or servility. However weakened by custom, the stigma of subordination persisted. Those who fled, or threatened to flee, their tenancies at Caldes, Llagostera, Font-rubí, Ribes, and Argençola, were those who clung to the honor of freedom. And in another sense of this concept they well understood, they had lost their "honors." Guilelm de Sant Martí was charged with seizing honors, including those of *Arnal Bunucii* and *A. de Plano,* in the Llobregat vills.

17. F2-3141, Ca2-3474.

At Cabra *Arnaldus de Muntfred* and *Petrus de Ual irana* both lost their honors to Bertran de Vilafranca, who drove them from the place.[18]

The dishonor of violence injured people in their persons as well as their property. It was not just that possession of an honor could be an excuse for a seizure, such as *Petrus Gitard*'s loss of 9s. in the Ribes valley. More remarkably, one of the memorials from Font-rubí speaks of people there being "dishonored" through bodily affliction. There are three telling items, clear enough in their import if not quite in every word. Dating from the early years of King Alfons, these complaints depict Berenguer de Bleda and his castellan (and their men) imposing carrying services on the villagers "as if on captives . . . and he pulls our beards and beats us badly. . . ." His castellan cuts our trees, requisitions our houses, demands provisions, "and they dishonor us and our wives. . . ." *Bernad Guilabert* lacked the donkeys demanded by a certain bailiff, so "he took two horses away from him and one plowshare and looted his house and dishonored him and beat him . and Guilelm de Grasbuac came and took away donkeys and (?) sacked his house and took off what he wishes, and beat him and persecuted [*encalzauit*] him as far as La Granada." One *Ferriol* suffered likewise at the hands of Berenguer de Bleda, who "dishonored him" and compelled him to buy . . . [illegible]."[19]

Here for once—and no other memorial refers so explicitly to "dishonor"—the shame and resentment provoked by petty violence come into the open. Ejection from honors was not confined to Font-rubí, it is true, and the "dishonoring" of people even there may refer to losses of property. But these men had their beards pulled (or pulled out? or cut?) and their wives "dishonored." Two things, that is. To begin with the second one, does this mean that the oppressive men under Berenguer de Bleda and his castellans

18. G3451, Ca2-3474.
19. R1-3433, F3-3288.

harassed women sexually or defiled them? How can I doubt it, given all else that was alleged at Font-rubí? The entreaties to the Lord-Princes reverberate with outrage. Moreover, it is uniquely in Catalonia that medieval peasants are known to have alleged that lords demanded to sleep with their brides on the first night. In 1462 the lords gave up any such presumption, while expressing doubt that the allegation had merit. Yet even if the recollection of occasional outrages fell short of describing the force of custom, for the practice as such was not counted among the "bad usages," this was a smoky scene; and in 1486 the Sentence of Guadalupe, which put an end to a massive civil war, included an express renunciation of the "right of the first night."[20]

Such a grievance may not have been new in the fifteenth century. Sexual oppression quite possibly figured in the housebreakings reported at Gavà, Cabra, and Argençola, as well as at Font-rubí. But only at Font-rubí was it reported in the euphemism of shame; only there can I regard it so much as a probable element of the afflictive violence people deplored. A century later peasants responding to Saint Louis' penitential investigations in Languedoc commonly alleged that their tormentors exploited suspicions of sexual misconduct to extort money.[21] Was there then some reticence on the part of our Catalonian scribes? People had no difficulty signalling transgressions against women, such as the mother at Terrassa who had a tooth knocked out, or the women whom Berenguer de Castellvell allegedly abused, cutting off the nose of one of them.[22] But the subtext of honor or its breach seems lacking in most of these representations.

With the abuse of men's heads and facial hair it was different. The beard is known to have signified dignity, freedom, and honor

---

20. Freedman, *Origins of Peasant Servitude in Medieval Catalonia,* p. 193; Alain Boureau, *Le droit de cuissage: la fabrication d'un mythe (XIIIe–XXe siècle)* (Paris, 1995), with special attention to pp. 264–267.

21. *HL,* vii, 19, 85, 124, 128, 133, 138, 160.

22. Ter3275, Cast3509.

in medieval culture. "To cut or pull a man's beard," Giles Constable has written, "was a grave affront unless it was part of a recognized ceremony." Beard-pulling as insult is attested in the *Deeds of the Counts of Barcelona,* a text composed by monks of Ripoll in the very years of our memorials; and in the Castilian *Poema del mio Cid* of perhaps a few years later.[23] Pulling "our beards" was explicitly associated with "dishonor" at Font-rubí. Moreover, in three of the memorials, two from Font-rubí and another from Castellvell, it figures as an element of characteristic petty brutality. The people of Font-rubí said that Pere dels Archs not only imposed arbitrary taxes, broke into their houses, and seized animals and produce; he also "binds us by our throats and pulls out our beards. . . ." On another occasion, Pere "broke into our houses and pulled out our beards and took our clothes." It must have been several years later that Berenguer de Bleda or his men pulled beards and beat the people who felt, as they said, "like captives." Beard-pulling was also charged against Berenguer de Castellvell, who ousted a worker from his manse, beating him, and leaving his manse waste. Is it significant that these allusions to beard-pulling come from adjoining domains in the upper Penedès region? Could it have been so local a custom? Anyway, beard-pulling goes together with beatings and seizures by the throat, which, taken separately, are more widely

23. Giles Constable, "Beards in History," introduction to *Apologiae duae: . . . Burchardi, ut videtur, abbatis Bellevallis apologia de barbis,* ed. R. B. C. Huygens. Corpus Christianorum continuatio medievalis 62 (Turnhout, 1985), p. 62; *Gesta comitum barcinonensium,* ed. Louis Barrau Dihigo and Jaume Massó Torrents. Cròniques catalanes 2 (Barcelona, 1925), p. 3; Stith Thompson, *Motif Index of Folk Literature . . . ,* rev. ed., 6 vols. (Bloomington, 1955–58), v, P672. For recent discussion of the cultural meaning of hair, see C. R. Hallpike, "Social Hair," *Man,* n.s., iv (1969), 256–264; and Dean A. Miller, "On the Mythology of Indo-European Heroic Hair" (unprinted? I owe this reference to Professor Rodney Needham); and with notable resonance with the Catalonian examples (and my thanks to Carroll Bisson for the reference), William Sayers, "Early Irish Attitudes toward Hair and Beards, Baldness and Tonsure," *Zeitschrift für Celtische Philologie,* xliv (1991), 154–189.

attested in rural Catalonia. *Raimundus Uldrici* and *Raimundus de Canneto* of Terrassa were perhaps in no state to fuss about beards when they were struck on their heads! At Corró, Pere de Bell-lloc was said to have bound men by the throat before throwing them in prison.[24]

Such abuses of the head, at least, may safely be regarded as a dishonoring form of violence. "A physical affront is a dishonour, regardless of the moral issues involved," creating a need for satisfaction.[25] Having one's beard pulled was not the only way to shame in the villages. People appealed to the Lord-Princes to remedy insults as well as injustice. Indeed, they felt themselves in solidarity with the troubled ruler, sharing the violation of estate like stigmata. The "great injury of the Lord-Count and his peasants" at Caldes and Llagostera has the appearance of dishonor as well as of economic loss. The expostulations from the Ribes valley and Font-rubí seem likewise to point to the shameful diminution of the comital domains, to "dishonoring" once again in that literal sense.

Yet the violence suffered and commemorated cannot always have damaged people's sense of worth. It is not easy, in the mostly formulaic entries, to discern when it did or did not. Were the seizures reported in large numbers at Caldes and Llagostera personally demeaning? Does the scribal shorthand—from *Guilelmus Lubet* 4[s.], from the son of *Poncius Guiriberti* 2[s.], and so on—conceal diverse stories diversely affective and humiliating? Surely the people at Terrassa, Caldes, Llagostera, and the Ribes valley remembered the seizures they reported as routine as well as injurious, their feelings preempted by the banality of petty tyranny. Moreover, a whole class of allegations seems to suggest that honor was felt generally to equate with status. In the Ribes valley it was a common complaint that Raimund de Ribes had exacted payments of security. *Petrus Arnad* said that Raimund "compelled me to confirm

---

24. F1-3409, F3-3288, Cast3509, Ter3275, Co3214.
25. Pitt-Rivers, *Fate of Shechem*, p. 5. Also *Usatges de Barcelona*, 5, 13.

right [*firmare directum*] . and he took 5s. from me." He "took 12s. from me *Iohanes Gili* because I had confirmed right to him, I don't know why."[26] These two men had been forced to secure their own appearances before Raimund on charges unspecified, although it seems that only *Iohanes* had the presence of mind to suggest that this was wrong. These are among the allegations that have suggested some tendency to involuntary compliance with the lord-vicar's arbitrariness in these remote upland vills.[27] But in most cases the aggrieved peasants were clear about the excuses for these payments, at once customary and deplorable. Similar demands were reported at Castellvell and Cabra as well as, more conspicuously, at Llagostera. One *Guito* said he had been compelled to pay 5 morabetins and on another occasion 20s., when pledged to others. Nor is this all. "When Arnal de Perella came to Caldes and Llagostera he put *Guito* in pledge for 50s. and took them [*all* those sous!] from him . and another time he put him in pledge for 10 morabetins and took 5 of them from him . and another time he pledged him to *Bernardus de Calle* for 7s. and took 3 of them from him. . . ."

These accounts, amplified in that of the persecution of *Guito,* are yet more evidence of a characteristic mode of lordly power, of jurisdictional power, that is in fact widely attested in twelfth-century societies. I cite them here to suggest that in rural Catalonia the power to exact securities was that of a social status jealous of its honor, or at least of its pretense to exploit this vestige of ancient public authority; one realized such power by exploiting it, thereby defining the honor of such lordship. "A peasant *Iohanes Oliba* appealed to the King . and so R. de Ribes took 40s. from him and struck him at the church door."[28] In this perspective the reactions of affronted peasants can likewise be made sense of. Their honor was virtually that of free men, although it can hardly have been a test of that freedom. The people of Ribes and Queralbs were more

26. R2-3217.
27. Above, pp. 102–104.
28. R1-3433.

nearly subject to customary obligations than those of Font-rubí or Cabra, yet I view it as no more than an accident of representation in our handful of written memorials that the evidence of beard-pulling comes mostly from Font-rubí. Nevertheless, there was less of shame than of sorrow in the memorials of Ribes, with only a hint of a lordly honor these peasants lacked the power to infringe. And what should be said of the "sold" men and women at Caldes de Malavella and Llagostera, the most enigmatic social evidence of all? If these people were all so branded by reason of debt, as can be confirmed only for *Petrus Amallus'* wife, they might well have lost the honorable status that imparted bite to the remonstrances else-where. Perhaps the most vivid evocation of shaming pressure on such status is found in the resentful recollections of peasants at Font-rubí. Some felt violated in demands for hospitality, "like slaves"; others driven "like captives" in carrying services; and one of them was represented as "persecuted" in a verb (*calcare*) that distantly echoes the ancient trampling of the vanquished in what became an imperial ritual of triumph.[29]

★ ★ ★

A distant echo, attenuated. Like other traces of these people, whose names, voices, and—finally—losses seem to be all they have left to us. It is little better than a guess that their material cultures were sturdier than their imaginative ones. I do not know what they created or sang or whether the coverlets and towels *Vital* lost at Caldes de Malavella and *Pere Oler* (and others) at Argençola were decorated. Their habitats lay close by the lands of the old Peace and Truce of God and of churches whose altar frontals were being painted and their apses frescoed in traditional scenes of a suffering faith. Their values, their sexual attitudes, their symbolisms largely elude us. I can only conjecture that delousing, with all its attendant

29. F2-3141, F3-3288. Cf. Michael McCormick, *Eternal Victory: Triumphal Rulership in Late Antiquity, Byzantium, and the Early Medieval West* (Cambridge, 1986), pp. 57–58, 144–145.

gossips and intimacies, was as central to rural sociability in down-land Catalonia as in the sheepherding vills of the Pyrenees.[30] What we know of these peasants' resentments, outrages, and sorrows rings truly, like clanging resonant bells, yet defeats all my efforts to individualize the voices heard by the scribes. If the scribes heard sympathetically what they wrote down, it is hard to be sure how well they understood it; how far they shared in the cultures to which they gave expression.

Was their own applied literacy a culture in itself? Or no more than a formulaic veneer? My inquiry intersects with evidence of a literate accountability at the very moment when economic constraints were forcing propertied people to commemorate in new ways, to interpret and persuade as well as to itemize. Ponç the Scribe was himself engaged in experimental work for the Lord-Count of Barcelona that resulted in an accountancy of audits and balances in the later twelfth century.[31] Whatever the perplexities of the village cultures, I can be sure that he and the other persons who wrote our memorials had been drawn out of their natal manses to live with canons or monks; some may have been city-bred, although little in the experience of people serving the rulers and clergies would have differentiated them from peasants. Not even their literacy, after all, which was that of a traditional and diluted legal culture more devoted to abstract possession than to practical circumstance, can have secured them distinction. What cannot be doubted is that their humanity was also that of their subjects.

The cries from suffering in the Ribes vills, at Font-rubí, and at Argençola survive in transmission, however distorted, because they

---

30. Cf. Le Roy Ladurie, *Montaillou: village occitan*, pp. 203–205; trans. Bray, pp. 141–142.

31. *FAC*, ii, nos. lB, 7, 8, 140, 141, 143; i, 49–59, 65–66. This shift is visible earlier and more clearly in Catalonia than elsewhere; cf. Alexander Murray, *Reason and Society in the Middle Ages* (Oxford, 1978), pp. 169–170, 183–184, 194–197; M. T. Clanchy, *From Memory to Written Record: England, 1066–1307*, 2d ed. (Oxford, 1993), pp. 92–96, 267.

were understood. Those from Caldes, Llagostera, and—again—
Font-rubí were narrated (however distorted) with rare power. The
pitiless portrait of Arnal de Perella; the terse characterization of his
bailiffs, one of whom "was rich and is now a poor man," the other
the reverse; the raw emotion in the representations of the needy
oppressed in Ribes and the deprived in Argençola: is all this not an
anonymous art to be likened to the sculptures in the cloisters of
Estany, Girona, and Sant Cugat?[32] A rhetoric of persuasion? Even of
compassion? If only we could know whether the written words
gave comfort to any as well as appealing momentarily to some!
What is certain is that no written genre beckoned to these scribes,
that peasant suffering lacked epic meaning, and that the artful passion that informed some of the memorials was expected to perish,
so to speak, at nightfall. Parchments might preserve the memory of
rights and claims; culture was made of stories, which are lost. Expressive, enticing, the memorials bring me close, as if to the ropes
of a forbidden *chantier,* then gently hold me away. ". . . And he is a
good accuser of wretched people. And he does many evil things in
the land with his lord Arnal."

32. See the photographs in *CR,* xi (1984), 220–236; v (1991), 119–128; and
xviii (1991), 169–180.

[V]

EPILOGUE

How much is surely concealed behind these words—concealed even in this most brilliantly narrated of the memorials! "From *Petrus Iohanis* 14s. from the plea . . . from *Poncius* the clerk when he litigated with his brother . and they did battle. 30s." (Perhaps some thought that money well spent?) I sense obscurely the place of "accusations" in what was imputed to *Bernardus Viues* as judicial malfeasance. But the stories drop out as the names multiply: *Arnallus Rog,* *Guilelmus* "Hammerhead," *Dominicus Roi,* ". . . the sold daughter of *Bernardus Orucii* . . ." And at Terrassa and Argençola, more names and blows: *Petrus Guilelmi de Brugera* claiming 3s. and 3 mitgers of barley and that his wife was struck, while *Petrus de Caruiens* itemized the loss of his provisions and household effects: these declarations, like so many others in all the vills are devoid of the stories, shorn of them doubtless at the moment of interrogation, that gave them life. Is it wrong of me to cling to the names? Of *A. de Plano* and his mother, who lost their honor at Gavà; of *n'Aiculina d'Almenara* whose good horse was taken at Cabra? They too had stories to tell, or explanations, such as the scribes in the Ribes valley were less hesitant to retain. "Another time [Raimund de Ribes] took from him [*Petrus Pardines*] 12s. for a certain brawl he had with someone in the street. He took from the widow *Gitarda* 18 sheep, unjustly."[1]

The names, first and last. Of *Petrus Ferren,* who left his "big and fine vineyard" at Cabanyes and went to Tarragona.[2] Of *Amallus Raimundi* at Font-rubí;[3] of *Russel* and *P. Ualard,* who had parcels at Valmala. Because they are my story, these names and those of the oppressors, but chiefly of these people who looked to the famous Count Raimund Berenguer IV as their lord: *Rabascun* and his fellows at Terrats, *G. Isam* who owed 3 mitgers of grain for his land at *Pegeres;* and to the Lord-King Alfons: *Pages, P. de Valoria,* and the other "franchisal men" who lamented their "broken" manses at Corró; *Petrus Arnad* and *Bernardus Duran* at Queralbs;[4] the *Barbarossas* (perhaps brothers?) and other "people of Argençola" . . . Why should their history be neglected in favor of their oppressors? Has only the wielding of power a history, so that Guilelm de Sant Martí and Deusde and Arnal de Perella (and his bad bailiff) and Raimund de Ribes and the rest become heroes as well as villains in my reflections? There were plenty of that sort, conspicuous; let me not forget Berenguer de Bleda and his castellans nor Berenguer de Clariana, roaming his western serras. They and their likes, "the little tyrant[s] of his fields withstood," lurked everywhere about these domains; they imparted the impetus of demand and constraint that spelled memorable change in these habitats of rural life; yet they were far outnumbered by the people who bore the brunt of their demands and constraints. So in some sense the history of these five hundred plus peasants, for all their inert reticence, must take precedence; a history such as they had: that is, if I can grasp it, for of course I impose it, without having it crumble in my hands. It is a fragile history, from the study of which I am left with one

1. R1-3433.
2. E–G29.
3. F1-3409.
4. R2-3217.

reasonably secure conclusion together with two problematic corollaries; an affirmation and two questions.

★   ★   ★

What seems certain in the end is that the peasants on the old public domains of Catalonia were experiencing a crisis of power in the middle of the twelfth century. Several of the memorials, those from Corró and Font-rubí, point to this fact explicitly. Pere de Bell-lloc was represented as violating the status of the "freed men" of Corró when he raided and imprisoned them. The people at Font-rubí made even clearer that the new taxes exacted by the Count and his castellans were such as "we never had in [your] father's lifetime." In truth, all the memorials represent the demands and violence inflicted on peoples of the Count or the King as disruptive and painful breaches of acceptable custom. And it is clear from countless other records that the arbitrary methods of constraint alleged and deplored in my selection of memorials were becoming general in lordships of all sorts in twelfth-century Catalonia. This is why the Lord-King and his prelates set out resolutely to oppose this habitual violence, first in the 1170s in remodeled statutes of the old Peace and Truce, and later by stronger measures of enforcement. The fierce opposition of magnates to this program not only marks the ignominious origins of a parliamentary opposition in Catalonia but also clinches the argument for a general crisis of power in that land in the twelfth century. The memorials of complaint from franchisal peasants are an early demonstration of that crisis—that is, of the makings of a critical showdown between radically opposed visions of right order in society—but the argument rests also and chiefly on other and vastly more abundant evidence.

What happened in the fiscal domains toward 1140–1160 was an ominous rumbling. Men like Deusde and Raimund de Ribes, themselves used to the harsh methods by which lesser barons had built up lordships in the past century, were rewarded for their fidelity by being put in charge of—but, no, let me say it more exactly: by being permitted to assume the Count's lordship over— major domains of the prospering backcountry. "Put us [back] in your lordship," pleaded the men of Font-rubí to Raimund Berenguer IV, "and keep us there!"[5] It was the abuse of that lordship by Berenguer de Bleda and his castellans that they denounced. Jacking up customary dues and tempted to exploit commended judicial privileges, such men aroused a futile petty resistance that was easy to squash by intimidation and affliction. This was a crisis of accountability given expression in complaints which resembled contemporary records evolving from *capbreus* to fiscal accounts of balance and receipt; a crisis which, in respect to the excess of arbitrary behavior over responsibility, was in process of resolution by the 1170s. The peasants of these old domains suffered and denounced a form of bad lordship from which they had been exempt and asked for redress. Scribes of the Lord-King's court surely had their appeals in mind when they devised a new fiscal accountancy. On the other hand, while I found some correspondance between the memorials and subsequent privileges, it looks as if the momentum of exploitative lordship was hardly checked. Whatever the exemptions, "bad customs" were becoming familiar even in the King's domains toward 1200.

So it would be mistaken to measure the significance of this crisis by its consequences. The troubles of the mid-twelfth century in comital (-royal) domains may be thought of as a first skirmish in a great conflict, but that cannot have been what mattered in their own day. They were symptomatic of pressures on benign traditional lordship such as had been in retreat almost everywhere in Catalan-speaking lands of old settlement.[6] And the real problem of

5. F1-3409.

6. Coral Cuadrada, *El Maresme medieval: les jurisdiccions baronals de Mataró i Sant Vicenç/Vilassar (hàbitat, economia i societat, segles X–XIV)* (Barcelona, 1988), pp. 642–643, rejects my view of a critical phase of pressure on traditional lordships. But she does not address my evidence and arguments in detail, nor does her

this meaning is how to measure the discontent recorded in the memorials in human terms. Were there norms of right order such as to explain the mediated responses that have come down to us? Can I posit a "moral economy" of Catalonian peasants such as James C. Scott proposed for southeast Asia: some balance of economic justice and tolerable exploitation?[7] The answer to such questions can only be "possibly." There has been no question here of rebellion. The favored response to brutality seems to have been flight: a rather massive exodus from Caldes de Malavella and Llagostera plus individual expulsions from manses in Ribes, Cabra, and Argençola. Nor was economic subsistence a collective issue, even if some people pleaded poverty. Yet I think the memorials are consistent enough in their implied norms to invite reflection on two problems more deeply engaged with the historical meaning of the crisis: namely, violence and suffering. Both problems have been broached above in their contexts of people and power. Both haunt me to the end, become destinations of my journey in the memorials.

Violence?

In some sense, violence was what all the people deplored. Adalbert "took" a pig away from *Petrus Uedre* at Gavà; *Raimundus Uldrici* of Terrassa suffered blows to the head; Bertran de Vilafranca seized an honor from *Petrus de Ual irana* at Cabra; men unnamed had their beards pulled at Font-rubí and Castellvell; while countless seizures of grain, money, and lesser valuables were registered everywhere. Always it was strong men (and sometimes women) forcing weaker

---

own case study disprove them. It will take more regional studies such as hers to show how baronial lordships bordering the comital domains fared in the later twelfth century. My study of 1985 is, in any case, revised and amplified in this book.

7. James C. Scott, *The Moral Economy of the Peasant*, chs. 5–7.

people against their wills. This is why the memorials must be labeled accounts of violence.

Violence is the story they tell—for the memorials if not always
their authors have also their stories. But can these be trusted? I have
tried to discern the subjective elements of these narrations, tried to
understand Guilelm de Sant Martí in his characteristic wrath so
unlike the calculating and pretentious Arnal de Perella, who for his
part resembled Raimund de Ribes only in his cynical manipulation
of justice. But my profiles move in a shadowed half-light. They rest
partly on equivocal words meaning "take" or "take away" as well
as "rob" (*tollere, abstulere*), making it difficult to measure injuries
and resentments in moral terms; moreover, they project bias or
even hostility beyond our power to control yet such as might alter
our grasp of the meaning of violence in specific cases. Suppose it
were given to me to learn that the dispossessions of *Arnallus Bonucii*
at Gavà and *Bernardus de Ualle spinosa* at Cabra were incidents of
local conflict rather than wanton acts of bad lordship? Would not
that lesson limit my estimate of the injuries such violence inflicted?
If so, a more dismaying requirement might seem to follow, that of
reassessing all recorded incidents of coercion and destruction on a
scale of least to worst, perhaps variously on principles dantesquely
moral or socially instrumental. For the evidence that binds me is at
the mercy, so to speak, of the observer as distinct from perpetrator
and victim; and "the observer's view," as William Ian Miller has
written, "is richly situated culturally, historically, and normatively"
to bring out "the relevant social norms and cultural competence by
which the action will or will not be comprehended as violent."[8]

So there would seem to be cause for caution in accepting the
appearance of violence in the memorials of complaint. Perhaps the
more so for the fact that the parties to those complaints did not
speak of "violence" as such. Not once. It is almost as if the scribes

---

8. William Ian Miller, *Humiliation and Other Essays on Honor, Social Discomfort,
and Violence* (Ithaca, N.Y., 1993), p. 59.

had wished to save me the trouble of persuading scholars who have become skeptical about the possibility of representing violence truthfully. And I would happily take refuge from the latters' censure if I thought that this microhistory from rural Catalonia met the tests of their well founded critique. One of their strictures arises from the suspicion, by no means new in historical study, of accounts of violence that are transparently the work of self-serving monks and clerks in the eleventh and twelfth centuries. They also question attributions of violence which seem to imply a political standard of normative, violated order.

The first of these considerations hardly applies to the present history. Although the memorials were doubtless written by clerics, they are in no way defensive of clerical interests. It was far from Arnal de Perella's worst misdemeanor that he harvested grapes in a vineyard in which Saints Mary and Stephen of Caldes de Malavella had tithes. Other churches were scenes of blows or seizures in the Ribes valley and the lordship of Castellvell, but these were represented as injuries to God's lay people. First objection dismissed. But how can I justify my contention that the memorials of complaint tell of "violence" even without using that word? Am I not succumbing to the very illusion castigated by the new school of "dispute resolutionists" by presuming the existence of a normative order in which authority protected life and property by resort to justice? It all seems so naïve, when put in this way.[9]

But the problem should not be put in this way. Even if I grant that the acts I label "violent" are subjectively so labelled (as I do) and that the voiceless tormentors might have remembered events differently (as I do), I am left with an impression of the allegations uneasily at variance with the approved model of a "stateless soci-

9. In addition to William Miller, I refer to Stephen D. White, Patrick Geary, Dominique Barthélemy, and others engaged in innovative work on law, power, and property in medieval Europe. See White, "The 'Feudal Revolution': Comment 2 [Violence in the Eleventh Century]," *Past & Present,* no. 152 (August 1996), pp. 205–223, with my "Reply," no. 155 (May 1997), pp. 208–225.

ety." To explain this I must return for a moment to my own experience with the parchment records. As I have repeatedly reflected on these pieces, they have seemed progressively to lose something of their impact. I begin to remember their relentless recitations as overstatements, even as rhetorical flights, in a world where seizures, intimidations, and distraints were too normal to warrant any more interest today than they did eight centuries ago. But this I believe to be a misreading induced by recently devised preconceptions about the normality of violence in stateless societies. I have no wish to deduce the nature of a society from sixteen documents, but neither do I wish to impose a theory ill suited to evidence which has been overlooked by historians and theorists alike. I had only to reread the documents seriatim to be struck—yes, that *is* the word—struck forcibly, and repeatedly, by their original power to evoke the shocking experience of blows, seizures, dispossessions, and intimidations; the coercing, to repeat, of the weak by the strong. The memorial of Caldes and Llagostera, all but quivering in suppressed rage, seems finally to detail the veritable destruction of prosperous rural settlements.

Moreover, it becomes irrefutably clear upon rereading that the peasants and scribes invariably felt, or said they felt, the blows, seizures, dispossessions, and intimidations as wrongful disruptions, as arbitrary and painful breaches of order. One last time let me call the roll, in the words of those who suffered, heard, and reported. Guilelm de Sant Martí "broke the village of Gavà and Sant Climent and Viladecans and forcibly took away donkeys." At Terrassa Deusde "broke a tooth" from a woman's mouth and hit *Raimundus Uldrici* and *Raimundus de Canneto* on the head. Arnal de Perella "did and does many evils to the Lord Count and his peasants" at Caldes and Llagostera. Less brutal but more insidious than those at Gavà and Terrassa, these evils—shirking the Count's service, appropriating produce to his own uses—were no less disruptive. Arnal failed to do justice when *Vitalis* of Llagostera was killed by one of the German knights he had been compelled to lodge. He drove people

out of both villages. He and his men did "great injuries" to the
Count. The "commemoration of misdeeds" perpetrated by Berenguer Mir at Esclet and Ganix details agrarian encroachments and
destructions. The incomparably indignant and eloquent appeals
from the people at Font-rubí spell out the implicit view that an old
customary order of comital lordship had been intolerably disrupted
by new taxes, insulting seizures of property and lodgings, and distraints of service. The normal order of customary tenancy is well
defined in a "commemoration" for Valmala, with only some indications of excessive or injurious customs. Pere de Bell-lloc disrupted the freedoms of men at Corró by acts of brutal force.
Raimund de Ribes may have acted within the limits of customary
power by exploiting judicial contingencies harshly, but he also
seized vineyards and manses, "destroyed" a royal mill, extorted,
ransomed, and struck people: the widow *Gitarda,* the peasant *Iohanes Oliba,* and many others. At Cabra Bertran de Vilafranca and
his enemies traded accusations of a full array of impositions, seizures, dispossessions, and petty brutalities, which are represented
uniformly as breaches of right order. And at Argençola the "people," complaining to the King about all that Berenguer de Clariana
"and his knights had unjustly done to them," inventoried the losses
of what look to have been raids of depredation.

Let the tormented voices from Font-rubí speak for them all:
"Lord Count Raimund Berenguer, all these evils written in this
charter are pillages and groans and distraints and forced taxes . . .!"[10]
Is this not a definition of violence, the forced and shocking disruption of tolerable order? Could there be a better one that makes as
much sense to us as to these medieval villagers? So defined, violence took different forms: shaming, for example, as well as beating
or seizing. Let there be no quibble as to where violence begins or
ends on a variable scale of injury. No one claims verifiable objectivity here, merely compassionate common sense.

10. F1-3409.

One other reservation applies: the alleged perpetrators cannot have fully shared the consensus about violence. That is, while (I imagine) not denying the unpleasantness of seizures and blows, they would have sought to defend their conduct as customary or lawful; would have wished to to mark off and justify what they found expedient in violence. I believe, moreover, that the memorials provide some warrant for identifying specifically seigneurial forms of coercion; that in any case, to reverse my point in Chapter III, one should not look upon seizures, ransoms, and afflictive behavior as simply an overflow of bellicose habits into lordship. With two or three partial exceptions, the perpetrators of violence were not at war with their victims.[11] They wished to subjugate them. Their violent habits had already become a seigneurial institution in Catalonia, a means of exploiting power, of profiting, disciplining, and confirming domination.

Such behavior intruded upon, did injury to, a traditional structure of power. Springing as they do from the subjective experience of the oppressed, the complaints imply the existence of a cognitive consensus about peace and order. And in their representations of violence and expectations of justice, the people (it cannot have been the scribes alone) recognized a normative sphere of power starkly alien to the familial and lordly solidarities in which they were caught up. "State" may be too strong a term, but the people of this book were not a "stateless society."[12]

11. Partial or *possible* exceptions: G3451, Co3214, Ca2-3474?
12. I wish not to be misunderstood on this point. The recognition of normative order, or orders, other than that of the centralizing "state" is a profoundly important tenet of a new historiography inspired by the works of Otto Brunner and of legal anthropologists. I share this perspective with the scholars mentioned in n. 9. But I have speculated that the breakdown of public justice in the tenth and eleventh centuries (which I hold to be a demonstrable fact) precipitated a newly violent mode of lordship such as assumed the character of a normative order itself ("The 'Feudal Revolution'," *Past & Present*, no. 142 [February 1994], pp. 6–42). And what I find in mid-twelfth-century Catalonia is evidence not only in support of this argument but also that what may be termed normative public order like-

Suffering?

That is why they complained. Violated, then invited to denounce, they itemized, and sought redress. Someone at Queralbs, not the original scribe, added up the pecuniary losses alleged there and wrote at the bottom of the parchment: "So, sum: 692s."[13] A notation not without irony, seeing that the parchment had been torn, for this high cause, from a book of the Gospels. And proof in its way, however misleading, that the memorials were accounts rendered. Could the violence they recorded be so easily remedied? Were they not also accounts of suffering? That is, of losses beyond remedy; appeals to compassion?

Historians seem uneasy with suffering. They don't know how much pain it takes. People who claim to suffer put us off, those who suffer in silence are disqualified under Clio's rules, while those who massively suffer tax our powers of comprehension.[14] The people of this book (including the author) labor under all these handicaps at once. Even if I exclude from consideration the torments of deprivation and defective hygiene which my subjects shared with medieval peasants everywhere, I find it hard to measure their pain in itemized losses, such as at Terrassa, or in frustrated expectations. Doubtless they hoped for redress, expected little for their efforts, and recovered (it seems safe to guess) less than they expected, if anything at all. No judgments of redress have survived, which may be why we have the original complaints in the first place. The discomforts were many, the representations problematic. Yet the

---

wise survived the crisis of the eleventh century. I believe this was characteristic, and indeed general in Europe, in the age of John of Salisbury. Lordship was not the only "order" or "culture" of power, in a time of difficult and creative adaptation.

13. R2-3217.

14. See the essays gathered under the title "Social Suffering" in *Daedalus,* cxxv (Winter 1996), especially those by Arthur Kleinman and Joan Kleinman, David B. Morris, Lawrence L. Langer, and Paul Farmer.

"groans" come through, and not only those from Font-rubí; come through perhaps all the more resonantly for being mediated by sympathetic auditors not given to overstatement.

As a rule the scribes leave me to imagine the pain or suffering resulting from seizures, exactions, dispossessions, or beatings. The "breaking" of heads and teeth at Terrassa pass without comment, as if so many items of indebtedness in a *capbreu*. So does the brutality at Corró, where Pere de Bell-lloc savaged houses, bound and dragged people to prison, and threatened to gouge out *Guilelmus Iohanis*'s eyes. But the items for Caldes and Llagostera assumed a uniquely different coloration in the prefixed narration of troubles. Here for once I can make out some alternation of partisan grumbling and compassion. Resentful of the self-promoting works of Arnal's bailiffs, the author branded them as injurious to the Count and his peasants and urged that the bailiwicks be restored to the old bailiffs. But he also lamented the broken oaths, disorders, and abusive accusations that had left the people "miserable" and caused more than half of them to flee to other lordships. Arnal de Perella threw people out of their vills: *Raimundus Guilelmi* and his sons from Caldes after having relieved them of 9s.; *Archimballus, Dalmacius Conilii* and his brother, with many others, from Llagostera. There was suffering in these places, in this violence, more than can be measured in the itemized seizures. On the excuse of the Count's expedition to Almería, Arnal took 20s. from *Nonar*'s son, "and his manse remains deserted."

Everywhere blows, seizures, shame, and pain in the variable styles that seem to portray the petty tyrannies of delegated lordship. But in some domains the bitter experience of power takes on a compassionate inflection in the representations of individual losses. In the Ribes valley almost every allegation comes with justificatory verbiage, some of which, as I have suggested, betrays a certain acquiescence in the judicial or customary excuses for exploitative demands. What is also striking is how these depictions evoke affective sympathies by spelling out personal consequences. Here the deserted manse is humanized. *Felix* the Peasant had two cows taken because his brother's wife died sterile "and so that manse was destroyed and is occupied by no one." Raimund de Ribes took away *Guilelmus Petri's* best ox "because of two cheeses which I had furtively received when I was hungry, so that afterward I could never work." *Petrus Raimundi* had a similar misfortune: fined the staggering amount of 94s. when his child-son died, he was forced to sell an ox, "and," he said, "I could not work any more." To be deprived of one's animals in these upland vales was to lose one's livelihood, to be thrust into poverty. Was the widow *Gitarda* so much better off that she could afford to lose—"unjustly"—eighteen sheep? Was she not close to them, like the Rachel luminously sculpted on a capital at Girona showing no fewer than eleven sheep with appealingly humanized heads? Something like pity sounds in these entries, the humane patience of a scribe caught up in the moral rhythms of the complaints he heard and wrote down.[15]

So the Ribes valley becomes a conservatory of rural emotion. There alone I can peer into the sufferings almost manse by manse, can recreate them as personal narratives. This is not proof of hardship worse than elsewhere, only of a sensitivity to human anguish that renders it rarely palpable. But the comprehension of individual distress was nowhere far submerged. *A. de Plano* and his mother had their honor seized at Gavà. Bertran de Vilafranca's hounding of *Arnaldus de Muntfred* at Cabra, though not explained, becomes brilliantly circumstantial in the story of threats to *Arnaldus's* daughter and son-in-law. And at Font-rubí, where donkeys were as critical to a microeconomy as were sheep in the Ribes valley, it is revealed for once that animals were subjects of humane pity. *P. Compan* grieved that he lent a mare to Berenguer de Bleda for threshing his grain, for "he treated the mare so badly that she neither ate nor drank until she died."[16]

15. R1-3433, R2-3217; see illustration titled "Rachel and her flock."
16. G3451, Ca2-3474, F1-3 (3409, 3141, 3288); final quotation from F2-3141.

This charge confirms my impression that the collective lamentations from Font-rubí, in some ways the most moving testimony of all, were compounded of individual tales of suffering. Suppressed as such in the first memorial, then sparingly but eloquently adduced in the second and third, these stories flow together in powerful expostulations to the Lord-Count. Not only *P. Compan* and *Martinus* (the one whose houses were requisitioned to his loss and shame), but many others pleaded for their Count's direct lordship and his "mercy." And went on pleading: if I could only read enough of its badly effaced words I would have counted the dorsal writing on memorial 6 as a fourth memorial from Font-rubí. These people suffered economically and physically; struggled to preserve their honorable status as customary tenants. At Argençola likewise the people joined to grieve over the forced exiles of their neighbors, including *Berengarius Maria* and his family, lamenting that they knew not where they had gone, but only that they had lost all they possessed.

The anguish survives in the voices, is what renders them audible. I do not wish to exaggerate the suffering conveyed in the fragile evidence of that emotion. The Count's and King's tenants survived, remembering two killings amongst their troubles. History knows of more desperate peasantries than these; and it may be that the societies here evoked belong to the troublous subset of peoples prosperous enough to be capable of protest when their lives are disrupted. What is peculiar (though surely not unique) to this Catalonian scene is the place of violence and fear in the disruption. If "violence" is conceived to encompass all that was forced unwillingly on the peasants of the memorials, then I may indeed be at risk of exaggerating their suffering. People *always* complain, *not* always persuasively. Moreover, the violence which stalks their representations, and caused their sufferings, was morally ambivalent, for it straddled a zone marking off conflicting customs of societal order. There was something familiar about the distraints visited on *Bertrandus* of Sant Climent, whose house was forced and a pig taken,

or on *Carbo,* when the lady Berenguera (and her men, be it understood) broke into his house at Font-rubí in pursuit of her "right."
Intimidations, ransoms, even quite possibly beatings would surely
have been defended as customary behavior by our voiceless perpetrators. Was there a subsistent strain of institutionalized violence left
over from ancient military practice?[17]

Nevertheless, the tenants of Count Raimund Berenguer IV and
his successor King Alfons I complained, and many of them complained bitterly, about the deportment of the men set over them
and their cronies. They represented that those people had disrupted
an old order of customary lordship. They said they were violated,
said that they suffered. I cannot read their memorials otherwise.

★ ★ ★

> The struggle of man against power is the struggle
> of memory against forgetting.
> —*Milan Kundera*[18]

So the paradox abides. In an agitated world of tumultuous lordships
some troubled peasants fought custom with custom, sought (as only
we can see it) to stave off a new mode of harsh exploitation that
made them feel, in words from Font-rubí, "like slaves." They were
the Lord-Count's (and Lord-King's) tenants, yet their story is
hardly one of distant masters, paragons of exaggerated virtue. That

17. G3451, F2-3141. Elisabeth Magnou-Nortier contends that the constraints
associated with "bad customs" are evidence of the continuity of Carolingian
military practice: see, e.g., "The Enemies of the Peace: Reflections on a Vocabulary, 500–1100," in *The Peace of God: Social Violence and Religious Response in France
around the Year 1000,* ed. Thomas Head and Richard Landes (Ithaca, N.Y., 1992),
ch. 3 (esp. pp. 69–79).

18. Mirek's words, in *The Book of Laughter and Forgetting,* tr. Aaron Asher (New
York, 1996), p. 4; but the obvious meaning of this aphorism which has lately
become widely current need not be all its meaning, as Kundera himself pointed
out, *The Art of the Novel,* tr. Linda Asher (New York, 1988), p. 130.

is why it was forgotten, first by those for whom the people were beneath remembrance, later by us who can only be excused as hard of hearing. What needed remembering was not so much how the Lord-Princes of Barcelona tended their old domains as how their people experienced power in their drenched and sun-baked rural habitats. For this experience is what they spoke of in words that we have, or almost have; what some ones once, momentarily, thought memorable, and what I have tried to read, to hear, to hold in the names and voices; in what we have of these people,—and all that we have.

The memorials of complaint and the very parchments which contain them were forged in that steamy experience of power. So they themselves, these artifacts, lead lives of their own, human-like lives insofar as they reveal the options and strategies of scribes groping uneasily between responsibilities and subjective engagement. They at least survive—and have more to tell the brave scholars who will one day decipher them more fully and edit them. Yet "I have travelled a good deal" in them myself, have come to know some of their dark corners well, even to recognize the authors— Ponç the Scribe and *Guilelm Ponç,* and the uneasy anonymous of Ribes—of two or three of them. They seem like reverberating spaces, holding echoing voices of scarcely more than audible accents. The memorials evoke the periphery of spoken rural life, an expressive yet confined zone in which event and recollection were rearranged by external prodding. It is a fated limitation of my little journey that the people I know best are the malefactors, but for whom there would be no records at all. Yet even of them—of Deusde, or rather his petty brutality; of Arnal de Perella and his wife and bailiffs building a lordship on the wreckage of comital power at Caldes de Malavella and environs; of Raimund de Ribes profiteering in justice in the Pyrenees; of the Berenguers exploiting the western settlements—even of these people the portraits lack depth.

Still less can the people subject to their power be realized. That is why I have clung to their names, and to the voices that come with some of them. *Maria Guitarda* of Caldes de Malavella, from whom Arnal de Perella took a 3s. pig; *Guilelmus de Nogér,* who fought unwarily with *Berengarius de Soler* at Ribes, which cost him a field; *Arnallus Oromir,* whose household at Argençola—perhaps quite a little one, yet including a woman's effects—was sacked: what have such people to prove of themselves but their faithful witness? What *they* might have wished to remember—their contented lives, their tolerably customary services and payments to the Count's or King's servants—are lost to all but conjecture from their yelps (for the *capbreus* tell us little more). They cannot be blamed for failing to answer questions they were never asked. For us they come on, these people, as they did to their interrogators, in their sheepish silences, yet also in their spoken sorrows, lamentations, and pleadings for mercy and justice. "Your man *Raimundus Marti*" and his fellows at Font-rubí, *Ramon Sunier* of the Ribes valley, who said that Raimund de Ribes took 200s. from his brother's killer, "and he himself [got] nothing." "And you, Lord, give us the land where we lived, that we may be yours [Font-rubí]!" The people of Cabra "dare not appeal" to the King "for fear of those knights . . . for you are far away and they are near us."[19]

Petrus Guilelmi de Brugera 12s. and 3 mitgers of barley . and [Deusde] struck his wife." *Arnallus de Valoria* of Corró, denouncing Pere de Bell-lloc. "*Ermessen* and my husband *Esbaldíd* 5s. because our small son died, no other cause." *Bernardus Burdo* weaver. *Giu* the clerk. *Pere Oler.* . . .

"For you are far . . . and they are near. . . ."

19. F1-3409, R1-3433, Ca1-2609.

Appendix 1

Usage, Citations, and Abbreviations

It is a minor inconvenience (in this work, that is; some today in Catalonia would put the matter more strongly!) that Raimund Berenguer IV (1131–1162) styled himself "Count" even after marrying the heiress to the king-dom of Aragon, and that their son Alfons I (1162–1196) remained "Count of Barcelona" even though he became "King of Aragon." I refer therefore to "comital" patrimony or domains even under Alfons I. I speak of "counts" or "count-kings" when referring to two or more of these rulers, or to none in particular; and of "Count" or (again capitalized) "Count Raimund Berenguer IV" when referring to him. Likewise, the "King" is specifically Alfons I (or Pere I, 1196–1213). "Prince" (or "Lord-Prince") is an alternative and authentic expression for Count or King.

Names

Those who "experienced power" in this book were chiefly those who complained of it, the comparatively weak and the many. I have wished not to generalize about them, but to commemorate them, even one by one, as they speak. To that end I have left them as if in holiday dress, have not translated their names down to modern parlance but have held them in the Latin finery their scribes imposed on them. Some of their names would have balked at translation anyway: *Carbo, Maienca, Guito.* Most names will be transparent even to readers unfamiliar with Latin: *Bertran-dus, Petrus, Raimundus.* A few others are easily explained: *Guilelmus* is the famous Frankish name commonly Anglicized as William (and we have also *Wilelmus*); *Iohanes* is John. All such names are printed in italic letter-ing.

On the other hand, I have modernized the names of men and women who were represented as exercising power in the villages. This is their book, too, and by the inexorable logic of power they are all too visible without typographic help. Their names are set out in Catalan forms somewhat modified for the convenience of non-Catalan readers: thus, I render *Berengarius* as Berenguer, the modern form; *Petrus* (Peter) as Pere; *Raimundus* as Raimund. But *Arnallus,* for example, is translated Arnal (not Arnau), *Guilelmus* as Guilelm (not Guillem).

Annotation

In what is primarily an essay of interpretation, I have held annotation to a minimum. The memorials, being described and enumerated in Chapter I and Appendix 4, are cited in notes only as much as seems necessary to specify which of the sixteen records is in question. They are cited according to an abbreviation combining letters and numbers. Thus, Ter3275 means the memorial of Terrassa, Archive of the Crown of Aragon, uninventoried parchments 3275; R1-3433 means first memorial of Ribes, ACA, uninventoried parchments 3433; and so on. The unique and remarkable memorial of Caldes de Malavella and Llagostera (C-Ll-2501, no. 4 of the series) seldom requires citation beyond my textual allusions; whereas the three memorials from Font-rubí and the two each from Ribes and Cabra might sometimes be confused without notation.

People spoke of obligations and losses in money and measures that are defined in the Glossary. The *solidus* (shilling or, in Catalan, *sou*), a money of account equivalent to 12 alloyed silver pennies, is abbreviated as s.; the penny (*denarius*) as d.

Abbreviations

ACA	Arxiu de la Corona d'Aragó (Barcelona)
BRABLB	*Boletín de la Real Academia de Buenas Letras de Barcelona*
CC	*Els castells catalans,* 6 vols. in 7 parts (Barcelona, 1967–79)
CPC	*Cartas de población y franquicia de Cataluña,* ed. J. M.

	Font Rius, 2 vols. in 3 parts to date (Madrid–Barcelona, 1969–83)
CPT	*Les constitucions de Pau i Treva de Catalunya (segles XI–XIII)*. Textos Jurídics Catalans. Lleis i Costums II/3 (Barcelona, 1994)
CR	*Catalunya romànica,* ed. Jordi Vigué, Antoni Pladevall, et al., 23 vols. in progress (Barcelona: Enciclopèdia catalana, 1984–95)
CSC	*Cartulario de "Sant Cugat" del Vallés,* ed. José Rius, 3 vols. Consejo Superior de Investigaciones Científicas (Barcelona, 1945–47)
DI	*Documentos inéditos del Archivo de la Corona de Aragón,* ed. Próspero de Bofarull y Mascaró et al., 42 vols. (Barcelona, 1847–1973)
FAC	*Fiscal Accounts of Catalonia under the Early Count-Kings (1151–1213),* ed. Thomas N. Bisson, 2 vols. (Berkeley, 1984)
HL	Claude Devic and J-J. Vaissete, *Histoire générale de Languedoc avec des notes et les pièces justificatives,* new ed., 16 vols. (Toulouse: Privat, 1872–1904)
LFM	*Liber feudorum maior. Cartulario real que se conserva en el Archivo de la Corona de Aragón,* ed. Francisco Miquel Rosell, 2 vols. Consejo Superior de Investigaciones Científicas (Barcelona, 1945–47)
perg. extrainv.	pergamins extrainventaris (uninventoried parchments)
R.B.	Raimund (or Ramon) Berenguer.

Appendix 2

Glossary

Trying to hear words in the voices, I have preserved much of the nomenclature and terminology as written in the twelfth century. This will not cause trouble, will help us visit that distant world. Some technical terms explained in the text are omitted here.

alberga(-ae)   Maintenance, in lodging, provisions. *See* p. 7.

Almoravid(s)   Berber Muslims who entered Spain in the later eleventh century and raided Catalonia.

alod *(alodium, alaudium)*   Property, patrimonial possession.

bachelors *(baculares)*   Probably young aspirants to honorable service or knighthood.

banal powers   Referring to *bannum,* the Frankish power of command.

benefice   Conditional tenure, or fief.

borda(-ae)   Half manse or small manse.

capbreu   Inventory of a lord's patrimony, specifying tenants' obligations and services. Term derived from Latin: *caput brevis,* "head of brief." *See* p. 4.

caput brevis (breue)   *See capbreu.*

castellan   Master of a castle, normally held in fidelity to a higher lord.

census   Rent, obligatory render to a lord.

clamores   Also *rancuras.* Written complaints required to institute judicial proceedings.

comital   Pertaining to the count.

count-kings   *See* Appendix 1. After 1162 the rulers in question were at once kings of Aragon and counts of Barcelona.

demesne (*dominicum*)   Direct lordship, what the Count or King (or other lords) exploited themselves, as distinct from fiefs.

dominicum, dominicatura   *See* demesne.

evangeliary   Book or manuscript bearing the text of the four Gospels of the New Testament.

familia   *See* family.

family   This word (Latin: *familia*) refers not only to immediate kin but also to the extended household, including servants, retainers, slaves, animals.

fief (*fevum*)   A tenure of lands or rights of lordship in return for service.

force(s) (*forcia, forcae*)   A general term for demands, constraints.

franchearii   Free, or freed, men.

honor (*honor*)   Patrimonial property or estate.

manse (*mansus*)   Homestead, rural tenure, house and farmland.

mitger   An Anglicized form of the Catalan *mitgera:* a dry measure, perhaps originally a half sextar.

morabetin   Muslim gold coin, valued at roughly 7s. (or 84d.).

mudejar   Muslim living under Christian rule.

Occitania   An artificial designation for the lands between the Pyrenees and the Rhône, later known as Languedoc.

Old Catalonia   Early settled lands east and north of the Llobregat valley, first so designated in the thirteenth century.

pagenses   Peasants.

parcellary   Referring to subdivided rural property.

pariliate   Land plowed by paired beasts.

puig   A small or steep hill, often fortified on top.

quarter   A dry measure.

querimonia(-ae)   Complaint(s).

quest (*questia, chestia*)   *See* tallage.

sextar   Normally a dry measure, perhaps originally one-sixteenth of the *modius.*

tallage   General term, derived from *tallia,* for an arbitrary (unconsented) tax. Normally synonymous with *questia* or *tolta;* perhaps also with *forca.*

tasc (*tasca, tascha*)   Share of produce, normally one-eleventh of crop.

testor (textor)   Weaver.

tithe   The biblical one-tenth of income paid to the church. Sometimes in hands of lay lords.

tolt *(tolta)*   Arbitrary tax or seizure.

vicar *(vicarius, vikarius)*   Officer appointed to exercise the Count's or King's justice.

Appendix 3

Aftermath: What Became of the Villages?

If the Lord-Count's villagers were given life by the memorials of complaint, there is little to show how, or how well, they survived in the flesh the crisis of the twelfth century. Some were driven from their homes, we know not where. Yet their villages, like their parchments, survived. Only not as well as the parchments. One can visit their places today, transformed though they are (more or less) by relentless modernity.[1] Or is it only places with the same names? Argençola may be the least changed in its remote rusticity, a few farmhouses scattered below the mouldering rubble of its castle. The vills of the Ribes valley live on, whereas the Roman and romanesque ruins at Caldes de Malavella compete weakly with the rattling business of bottled spring water. Corró, Font-rubí, Cabra: yes, their elevated sites still evoke the events we have visited, but of human construction all seems changed. As also in the Llobregat vills and Terrassa, swallowed up in the ravenous urban jaws of greater Barcelona. Yet these little places—taxed, judged, transacted—quite as surely left traces in the archives of king and churches as their peoples' voices sounded through the memorials of complaint. One day their later history beyond the limits of this book may be told.

What is certain is that the domains of the memorials, with their vills or castles, remained in the lord-kings' direct power. They were sometimes commended to baronial or castellan allies, seldom if ever alienated permanently. So the castellany of Terrassa, with or without the bailiwick, passed

---

1. They are listed in *Diccionari nomenclàtor de pobles i poblats de Catalunya,* 2d ed. (Barcelona, 1964); and *Gran enciclopèdia catalana,* 18 vols. (Barcelona, 1969–93).

to (and from) the families Claramunt, Montcada, and Muntanya; the functional successors to Deusde of Cardona.[2] Everywhere the king's protectorate seemed compromised already by 1200, when it was not yet clear that the royal domain would be a haven of peasant freedom. Yet when the people of the Ribes valley complained in 1252 that their castellans, including yet another Raimund de Ribes, had imposed uncustomary exactions on them, King Jaume I prohibited such demands.[3] Paul Freedman has found that allusions to redemption and bad customs became uncommon in royal lands in the thirteenth century. Then came the Black Death, depopulation, a tightening of the vice of rural lordship, and the decision of later kings to oppose *remença* serfdom.[4] I do not know which hearths in the royal domain were burdened with servile obligations in the fifteenth century. There must have been some. It is hard to believe that in that day the descendants of *Pere Oler* or *Maienca* or *Martinus de Fonte rubeo* remembered what had happened in the twelfth century. So much had happened since. Their villages had changed. They knew nothing of the old parchment memorials preserved in the royal archives. Nor (I suppose) did anyone else. The villages went on changing,—and forgetting. They still are. Like the rest of us.

2. *CC*, ii, 144–152.

3. Jaume Martí i Sanjaume, *Dietari de Puigcerdá amb sa vegueria de Cerdanya i sotsvegueria de Vall de Ribes,* i (in two parts) (Ripoll-Lleida, 1926–28), pp. 524–525 (no. 28).

4. Freedman, *Peasant Servitude in Medieval Catalonia*, chs. 4–7.

Appendix 4

The Memorials: A Register

The records on which this study rests have their human interest. I have conversed with them without pressing them for impertinent details. They are nonetheless artifacts in need of the expert attention that will enable historians one day to learn more from them and their likes about the speech, literacy, attitudes, furnishings, and experience of ordinary people who lived in the twelfth century. Even unprinted they are accessible to readers familiar with medieval records. The list which follows is meant to help such readers by describing the memorials more technically than in Chapter I. Editions known to me are cited; none is satisfactory.

1

(Undated. c. 1122–1138)

Recognition of the Count's alberga *in Terrats.* (Tts 3283)

ACA, Cancelleria, pergamins extrainventaris 3283 (carpeta 360). Original, parchment, 74 × 219 millimeters. Divided by AbCDEF. Reverse: No. 445. i0 Armí. de Manresa sach St. Ignasi. 2430.
Edited: Joaquín Miret y Sans, "Pro sermone plebeico," *BRABLB*, vii (1913–14), 108.

Lists the obligations of eleven householders. Specifies that the Count (of Barcelona) has only the indicated maintenance "and no other rent [*sensum*] at all."

2

(Undated: c. 1145–1150)

Infractions alleged against G(uilelm) de Sant Martí in Gavà, Sant Climent, and Viladecans. (G3451)

ACA, perg. extrainv. 3451 (carpeta 364). Original, parchment, 173 × 145 mm. Reverse: *.xxviiii . sac.* (later s. xii?). 2354.

Specifies seizures by Guilelm and Adalbert from some eleven persons. The two first entries are followed by a third hastier one, all in the hand I attribute to Ponç the Scribe

3

(Undated: c. 1145–1150)

"Complaints which the people of Terrassa make about Deusde to the Count of Barcelona." (Ter3275)

ACA, perg. extrainv. 3275 (carpeta 360). Original, parchment, 136 × 205/216 mm. Dorse: *Que[rimon]ia . . .* (later s. xii) . . . *[tera]cia* (effaced, s. xiii–xiv). 5_. Armí. de Tarragona sach M. No 77. 2460.

Lists Deusde's seizures from and other acts of violence against twenty-eight persons.

4

(Undated: c. 1150)

"Brief of many evils which Arnal de Per[ella] did and does to the Lord-Count and his peasants" at Caldes de Malavella and Llagostera. (C-Ll-2501)

ACA, perg. R.B. IV extrainv. 2501 (carpeta 41). Original, parchment, dry point lined. 425 × 303 mm. Reverse: continuation. *cabbreuium super maleficiis que fecit A. de . . .* [effaced] *a lacustaria* (s. xiii?).

A long list of alleged seizures and exactions by Arnal de Perella, his bailiffs, and even his wife, in the two villages. Extending to the reverse of the parchment, the items are preceded by a narrative account of Arnal's misdeeds.

5
(Undated: c. 1152-1160)
"Commemoration" of Ber(enguer) Mir's injuries to his Lord R. Berenguer, Count of Barcelona. (E-G29)

ACA, perg. R.B. IV sense data 29 (carpeta 41). Original, parchment, 219 × 92/95 mm. Reverse: . . . . *et cabbreve de E [. . .] et de lacostaria* (s. xiii?).

Three sets of entries in two hands, detailing seizures and encroachments by Berenguer Mir in the vills of Esclet and Ganix. *Guilelmus Ponci* attests to the truth of the allegations.

6
(Undated: c. 1150–1155)
Complaints by the people of Font-rubí to the Count of Barcelona relating to new taxes levied by the Count and to new impositions, seizures, and other violence by Berenguer de Bleda, the Lady of Mediona, and Raimund de Barbera. (F1-3409)

ACA, perg. extrainv. 3409 (carpeta 363). Original, parchment, 381 × 225/213 mm. Reverse: additions, or possibly a further memorial, very effaced (c. 1160): *Clamamus nos de berengarii de ipsa bleda quando accepit . . . & alia uice abstulit . . .* In another hand (s. xii or early xiii): *Querimoniae hominum fontis rubee.*
Edited: Miret y Sans, "Pro sermone plebeico," *BRABLB*, vii, 109–110, with many omissions and overlooking the dorsal matter.

A powerfully subjective and collective lamentation of uncustomary impositions and seizures.

7

(Undated: c. 1162–1165)

Complaints by the people of Font-rubí against Berenguer de Bleda and his castellans. (F2-3141)

ACA, perg. extrainv. 3141 (carpeta 357). Original, parchment, 103/109 × 276 mm. Effaced on lower right margin. Reverse: i2 Armí. de Montblanch sach María. no. ii28.

A more specific series of allegations on behalf of five individuals as well as the community, stressing exactions and seizures, and detailing the requisitioning of one *Martinus*'s dwellings.

8

(Undated: c. 1162–1172)

Complaints by the people of Font-rubí against Berenguer de Bleda and his castellan. (F3-3288)

ACA, perg. extrainv. 3288 (carpeta 360). Original, parchment, 113 × 336 mm. Mutilated on right. Reverse: *querimonie quod homines de fonterubeo habent / de berengario de bleda* (s. xii–xiii). ii. Armí de vilafrancha, sach St magí. No i92. 2441.

Strongly collective sentiments against increased pressures of lordship, "dishonoring," wasting of trees, and exploitative demands for service.

9

(Undated: c. 1150–1162)

"Commemoration of the land of Valmala which Dorca holds." (V3202)

ACA, perg. extrainv. 3202 (carpeta 359). Original, parchment, 197 × 84/86 mm. No dorsal marks. The first lines may arouse the suspicion that this piece has lost its right-hand margins, but it is clear from the rest that the text is preserved complete.

Refers to some thirty-two people under obligation to the Count, while asserting that some have "taken from" the Count.

10
(Undated: c. 1162–1170)
Four men of Corró (d'Avall) complain to the Lord King together with the other franchearii *about depredations by Pere de Bell-lloc.* (Co3214)

ACA, perg. extrainv. 3214 (carpeta 359). Original, parchment, 96 × 195 mm. Reverse: *Querimonie p*[. . . .] *podio uiride et aliorum* . . . (effaced, s. xiii?).

Allegations that Pere de Bell-lloc has broken into their vill, pillaged their houses, threatened them, and imprisoned them.

11
(Undated: 1162–c. 1170)
Complaints that Raimund de Ribes has seized, imposed on, and beaten people of the Ribes valley and Pardines. (R1-3433)

ACA, perg. extrainv. 3433 (carpeta 363). Original, parchment, 353 × 100/105 mm. Reverse: (across top, very effaced) *et sunt sol. dc xl.ii. et ꝥ .iii. [mas] et [. . . .]e et [. . . . . .] / et sol .xxx. / et s[unt . . .] omnia .ii. . . .* 2377.

This memorial refers to some thirty acts of violence, many suffered by named persons, expressed in a third-person voice. There are notations, indicating that the complaints were reviewed.

12
(Undated: 1162–c.1170)
Complaints that Raimund de Ribes has seized, imposed on, and beaten people of Queralbs. (R2-3217)

ACA, perg. extrainv. 3217 (carpeta 359). Original, parchment, 127 × 227 mm., cut from a s. xii evangeliary (at Matt. 20.18).

Refers to some twenty-two acts of violence suffered by named persons in a first-person voice.

13
(Undated: c. 1159–1166)
Complaints by Guilelm de Castellvell against Berenguer de Castellvell.
(Cast3509)

ACA, perg. extrainv. 3509 (carpeta 365). Original, parchment, 350 × 136/144 mm. Reverse: + 2312.

The Lord of Castellvell charges his castellan with a long series of violences against peasant women; seizures of a forge or shop (*fabrica*) at Castellvell, and of manses; unwonted impositions on peasants; and much else.

14
(Undated: c. 1173–1175)
Bertran de Vilafranca addresses King and Count Alfons I complaining of the malfeasance of Berenguer de Clariana and others at Cabra.
(Ca1-2609)

ACA. perg. Alfons I apèndix, extrainv. 2609 (carpeta 56). Original, parchment, 253 × 191 mm. Reverse: some five lines in same or early hand, effaced (see below). No. 276.
Edited: Miret y Sans, "Pro sermone plebeico," *BRABLB,* vii, 110–111; Frederic Udina, "Un singular pergamí del Rei d'Aragó, Alfons I, comte de Barcelona i marquès de Provença," *Provence historique,* xxiii (1973), 116–118.

Diverse charges of disruption by taxation, seizures, dispossessions. Bertran writes as (former?) bailiff, urging the Lord-King's indignation about the mistreatment of his men.

Udina prints the dorsal notation as follows: " (1) ne in paramentum vestrum et de patri vestri . . . et per forcia quantitate (?) (2) tolra si vos quia non detis et de Guillelmo de Concabella et mater sua et Berengario de Cleria (sic) (3) de una finina (sic) que habuit intestada .c. sous et de alia homo quo voccant . . . (4) qui erat in . . . ad alios .c. sous . . . partem, Domino Regio, .xx. sous in (5) alia (?) pignora nisi a Do (sic) Domino Regio . . . .i. . . . diner (?) .xi."

15
(Undated: c. 1173–1175)
Complaints by Guilelm de Concabella, Berenguer de Clariana, and the
Good Men of Cabra against Bertran de Vilafranca. (Ca2-3474)

ACA, perg. extrainv. 3474 (carpeta 364). Original, parchment, 35/106 ×
420 mm. Reverse: continuation of text. *Querimonias o Quexas* (s. xviii–
xix). 2274.

Very specific charges of dispossession, persecution, and fiscal exploitation.

16
(Undated: c. 1180–1190)
The people of Argençola joined by Berenguer de Aguiló complain to God
and the King of unjust treatment by Berenguer de Clariana and his men.
(A3145)

ACA, perg. extrainv. 3145 (carpeta 357). Original, parchment, 305 ×
210/216 mm. Mutilated. Reverse: *querimonie hominum* (s. xii–xiii?) *de*
argençola (added later). No. i053. i2 Armí. de Montblanch, sach <u>María.</u>

An inventory of household losses by twelve persons. The text continues
on the reverse, evaluating the losses at 10,000s. and looking to redress in
the Lord-King's court.

Further Reading

The study of Catalonian peasants and their anxieties lies in fields of learning deep and diverse; or at least I believe it should. My purpose in listing a few salient items in a vast bibliography is simply to orient readers who wish to read further. A select program in English could well be pursued in the works of Marc Bloch, Richard Koebner, Georges Duby, Peter Burke, Emmanuel Le Roy Ladurie, Carlo Ginzburg, Pierre Bonnassie, Paul Freedman, Robert Redfield, James C. Scott, and J. G. Peristiany, mentioned in that order below. The list includes, but also excludes, some works cited in the footnotes. Dates of first publication are in some cases given in square brackets.

Historical Perspectives

Modern research on medieval agrarian life owes much to Marc Bloch, *Les caractères originaux de l'histoire rurale française* (Oslo, 1931), of which an updated and amplified edition was published in 2 vols. (Paris, 1961–64), and an English translation by Janet Sondheimer, *French Rural History: An Essay on its Basic Characteristics* (Berkeley, 1966). See also Richard Koebner, "The Settlement and Colonization of Europe," *The Cambridge Economic History of Europe,* i, 2d ed. (Cambridge, 1966 [1941]), 1–91. More recent research on rural structures of settlement, habitat, power, and culture is well synthesized by Robert Fossier, *Enfance de l'Europe: Aspects économiques et sociaux,* 2 vols. Nouvelle Clio 17, 17bis (Paris, 1982); and Werner Rösener, *Peasants in The Middle Ages,* tr. Alexander Stützer (Cambridge, 1992); see also Jean Chapelot and Robert Fossier, *The Village & House in the Middle Ages,* tr. Henry Cleere (London, 1985 [1980]). A more nearly sociological view will be found in Karl Bosl, *Frühformen der Gesellschaft im mittelalterlichen Europa: ausgewählte Beiträge zu einer Strukturanalyse der mittelalterlichen Welt* (Munich, 1964). The historical dynamics of early medieval societies are brilliantly expounded by Georges Duby, *The Early Growth of the European Economy: Warriors and Peasants from the Seventh to the Twelfth Century,* tr. H. B. Clarke (London, 1974 [1973]).

The nature of culture in rural societies is well suggested by Peter Burke, *Popular Culture in Early Modern Europe* (London, 1978); and Roger Chartier, *Cultural History between Practices and Representations,* tr. Lydia G. Cochrane (Ithaca, N.Y., 1988); and illustrated with remarkable results by Emmanuel Le Roy Ladurie, *Montaillou: Cathars and Catholics in a French Village, 1294–1324,* tr. Barbara Bray (London, 1978 [1975]); and Carlo Ginzburg, *The Cheese and the Worms: The Cosmos of a Sixteenth-Century Miller,* tr. John and Anne Tedeschi (London, 1980 [1976]).

Mediterranean Studies

The works of Le Roy Ladurie and Ginzburg share wider Mediterranean contexts, both historical and anthropological. The concept of "encastellation" (*incastellamento*) as a characteristic structure of rural change was powerfully planted by Pierre Toubert, *Les structures du Latium médiéval: le Latium méridional et la Sabine du IXe à la fin du XIIe siècle,* 2 vols. Bibliothèque des Ecoles françaises d'Athènes et de Rome 221 (Rome, 1973). For its pertinence to Catalonia see Pierre Bonnassie, "Les *sagreres* catalanes: la concentration de l'habitat dans le 'cercle de paix' des églises (XIe s.)," *L'environnement des églises et la topographie religieuse des campagnes médiévales,* ed. M. Fixot, E. Zadora-Rio. Documents d'Archéologie française (Paris, 1994), pp. 68–79. Not only Caulers (near Caldes de Malavella: see the work of Manuel Riu cited in Chapter II, note 11) but also Esquerda (Osona, presumably near Valmala) has been the subject of remarkable archaeological research, in this case directed by Dr. Immaculada Ollich. See Imma Ollich i Castanyer, Maria Ocaña i Subirana, Maties Ramisa i Verdaguer, and Montserrat de Rocafiguera i Espona, *A banda i banda del Ter: Història de Roda* (Vic, 1995), and reports in *Acta historica et archaeologica mediaevalia* (Barcelona).

For León and Castile, see the valuable studies by Reyna Pastor de Togneri, *Resistencias y luchas campesinas en la época de crecimiento y consolidación de la formación feudal: Castilla y León, siglos X–XIII* (Madrid, 1980); and T. F. Ruiz, *Crisis and Continuity: Land and Town in late Medieval Castile* (Philadelphia, 1994).

Catalonia

The fundamental work on early medieval Catalonia is Pierre Bonnassie, *La Catalogne du milieu du Xe à la fin du XIe siècle: Croissance et mutations d'une société*, 2 vols. Publications de l'Université de Toulouse-Le Mirail. Série A 23, 29 (Toulouse, 1975–76). A useful assessment of this work may be found in Gaspar Feliu i Monfort, "Societat i economia," *Symposium internacional sobre els orígens de Catalunya (segles VIII–XI)*, 2 vols. Generalitat de Catalunya (Barcelona, 1991–92), i, 81–115. Together with Pierre Guichard, Bonnassie traced the structures of rural communities in Valencia and Catalonia in *From Slavery to Feudalism in South-Western Europe*, tr. Jean Birrell. Past and Present publications (Cambridge, 1991), ch. 8. On the problem of *remença* serfdom and its origins, the pioneering work of Jaime Vicens Vives, *Historia de los remensas en el siglo XV* (Barcelona, 1945) has been amplified and updated by Paul Freedman, *The Origins of Peasant Servitude in Medieval Catalonia*. Cambridge Iberian and Latin American Studies (Cambridge, 1991).

On matters of crisis and violence, see also Josep Maria Salrach, "Agressions senyorials i resistències pageses en el procés de feudalització (segles IX–XII)," in *Revoltes populars contra el poder de l'Estat* (Barcelona, 1992), pp. 11–29; Blanca Gari, "Las *querimoniae* feudales en la documentación catalana del siglo XII (1131–1178)," *Medievalia* v (1984), 7–49; and Pere Benito i Monclús, "Els *clamores* de Sant Cugat contra l'hereu del Gran Senescal i altres episodis de terrorisme nobiliari (1161–62)," forthcoming. On economy and culture, Coral Cuadrada, *El Maresme medieval: les jurisdiccions baronals de Mataró i Sant Vicenç/Vilassar (hàbitat, economia i societat, segles X–XIV)* (Barcelona, 1988); Flocel Sabaté, "Estructura socioeconòmica de l'Anoia (segles X–XIII)," *Acta historica et archaeologica mediaevalia* xiii (1992), 175–238; and Antoni Riera i Melis, "El sistema alimentario como elemento de diferenciación social en la alta edad media. Occidente, siglos VIII–XII," in *Representaciones de la sociedad en la historia: de la autoconplacencia a la utopía.* Instituto de Historia Simancas (Valladolid, 1991), pp. 8–62.

Comparative and Theoretical Perspectives

Robert Redfield, *Peasant Society and Culture: An Anthropological Approach to Civilization* (Chicago, 1956) is a standard discussion, to be supplemented by Eric R. Wolf, *Peasants* (Englewood Cliff, 1966), and *Peasants and Peasant Societies: Selected Readings,* ed. Teodor Shanin. Penguin Modern Sociology Readings (London, 1971).

On Mediterranean societies and their cultures, see *Honour and Shame. The Values of Mediterranean Society,* ed. J. G. Peristiany (Chicago, 1966), together with the works of Julian Pitt-Rivers and David D. Gilmore cited in Chapter IV, note 15. That peasant unrest takes varied forms is finely evident in James C. Scott, *The Moral Economy of the Peasant: Rebellion and Subsistence in Southeast Asia* (New Haven, 1976); see also Irwin Scheiner, "The Mindful Peasant: Sketches for a Study of Rebellion," *The Journal of Asian Studies* xxxii (1973), 579–591; and Michael Gilsenan, "Domination as Social Practice: Patrimonialism in North Lebanon: Arbitrary Power, Desecration and the Aesthetics of Violence," *Critique of Anthropology* vi (1986), 17–37.

The evidence treated in this book has a complex interface with current theoretical explorations of power and process. See the studies edited by Steven Lukes under the title *Power. Readings in Social and Political Theory* (New York, 1986), especially Georg Simmel, "Domination and Freedom," pp. 203–210; and Judith Shklar, *Ordinary Vices* (Cambridge, Mass., 1984), esp. ch. 1. Also Simon Roberts, *Order and Dispute: An Introduction to Legal Anthropology* (Harmondsworth, 1979); Pierre Bourdieu, *The Logic of Practice,* tr. Richard Nice (Stanford, 1990 [1980]); James C. Scott, *Domination and the Arts of Resistance: Hidden Transcripts* (New Haven, 1990); and William Ian Miller, *Humiliation and Other Essays on Honor, Social Discomfort, and Violence* (Ithaca, N.Y., 1993).

Index